DR YESHAYAHU (JES
—spiritual scientist,]
activist—is founder o
community in Hardu!
the Global Network for Social Threefolding,
director of Global Event College and contributor to the School of Spiritual Science. He is the author of *Cognitive Yoga*, *The Three Meetings*, *Jerusalem, The Twilight and Resurrection of Humanity*, *Spiritual Science in the 21st Century*, *The Spiritual Event of the Twentieth Century*, *The Event in Science, History, Philosophy & Art*, *The New Experience of the Supersensible*, *America's Global Responsibility* and *Cognitive Yoga: How a Book is Born*.

THE TIME IS AT HAND!

*Ahrimanic and Michaelic Immortality
and the Apocalypse of the Age of Michael*

Yeshayahu (Jesaiah) Ben-Aharon

TEMPLE LODGE

Temple Lodge Publishing Ltd.
Hillside House, The Square
Forest Row, RH18 5ES

www.templelodge.com

First published by Temple Lodge Publishing, 2024

© Yeshayahu Ben-Aharon 2024

The Publishers are grateful to Scott Hicks for his editorial work

This book is copyright under the Berne Convention. All rights reserved. Apart from any fair dealing for the purpose of private study, research, criticism or review, no part of this publication may be reproduced, stored in a retrieval system, or transmitted in any form or by any means, electronic, electrical, chemical, mechanical, optical, photocopying, recording or otherwise, without the prior written permission of the copyright owner. Inquiries should be addressed to the Publishers

The right of Yeshayahu Ben-Aharon to be identified as the author of this work has been asserted in accordance with sections 77 and 78 of the Copyright, Designs and Patents Act, 1988

A CIP catalogue record for this book is available from the British Library

ISBN 978 1 915776 12 9

Cover by Morgan Creative featuring a painting by Sylvia Waiblinger
Typeset by Symbiosys Technologies, Vishakapatnum, India
Printed by 4Edge Ltd., Essex

'To interpret the signs of the times, let us arrange our lives in accordance with these three mysteries of our time: the mystery of Michael, the mystery of Christ, and the mystery of Sorat.'

Rudolf Steiner,
lecture of 12 September 1924 (GA 346*).

---

* See p. 120.

Contents

Preface	1
Lecture 1 *Ahrimanic Immortality, the Matrix and* *Technological Singularity* Stuttgart, 3 November 2017	3
Lecture 2 *Michaelic Immortality* Stuttgart, 4 November 2017	28
Lecture 3 *The Two Apocalyptic Beasts and the Mystery of the Wound* Überlingen, 3 November 2022	55
Lecture 4 *Follow This Good Star* Überlingen, 4 November 2022	79
Lecture 5 *The Time is at Hand!* Überlingen, 5 November 2022	102
Quoted Volumes from Rudolf Steiner's Collected Works	120

Preface

On 13 January, 1924 Rudolf Steiner published the Foundation Stone Meditation in the Newsletter of the Anthroposophical Society. In the same day, the soul of Helmuth von Moltke, who had died in 1916, communicated through Rudolf Steiner the following words to his wife. In the spiritual world, the soul of Moltke already sees the twentieth century from its end backward, and tells his wife that before the end of the century the goals of the Christmas Foundation Conference cannot be fulfilled:

> Yes, if only this were heard: 'Practise spirit remembering', 'Practise spirit awareness', 'Practise spirit seeing'. But human beings will only hear it when the Michael spirit succeeds in finding in the astral light the trails leading to the spirit altar upon which burns the astral flame that Ahriman fears.
>
> No doubt this will take until the end of the century. For as yet the eyes are not there that could perceive the Christ walking in the ether light. Eyes filled with the discord at work in humanity will not be able to have such vision.[1]

The lectures included in the present book that were delivered in 2017 and 2022, form part of the practical work in the global School of Spiritual Science. This work intends to demonstrate that since the end of last century, some 'eyes *are* there that *do* perceive the Christ walking in the ether light', and that as a result of this perception, 'the Michael spirit *succeeded* in finding in the astral light the trails leading to the spirit altar upon which burns the astral flame that Ahriman fears'. This altar is the free etheric heart, and its fire can only be kindled through the new revelation of the etheric Christ. This takes place when

---

[1] Helmuth von Moltke, *Briefe und Dokumente zu Kriegsausbruch und Kriegsschuldfrage* (Perseus 2005), p. 291.

human beings unite their hearts in creative collaboration, to form the new Michaelic community through sacred enthusiasm, love and creative joy.

If we continue to form this community in the 20s, 30s and 40s of this century, some humans will be found who 'will hear it' because their eyes will not be blinded by 'the discord at work in humanity'. Their eyes and ears will be opened by the all-encompassing love and brotherhood, inspired by the etheric Christ, walking among us in His etheric form.

As I write this preface, we are celebrating the three great centenary events of the burning of the first Goetheanum on New Year's Eve, 1922, the Christmas Foundation Conference of 1923-4, and Rudolf Steiner's death on 30 March, 1925. This time is crucial, because we must be able to demonstrate that after a century some human souls have heard and answered the cosmic-earthly call of Michael and work together to actualize it.

The twenty-first century is the second, middle century of the three centuries of the present age of Michael, and it is the most decisive one. If humanity again misses the goal of Michael, it will be hardly possible to recuperate from it, and human evolution will be derailed for a long time. The present age of Michael can therefore rightly be called 'the Apocalypse of the age of Michael'. The most important goal of Michael in his present age is that the new revelation of the etheric Christ will be fully grasped, because the resurrection of humanity depends on this. This is the centre of the work in the School of Spiritual Science and the lectures included in this book can serve as introduction to *The Twilight and Resurrection of Humanity* and as an extension to some of its subjects.

Lecture 1

Ahrimanic Immortality, the Matrix and Technological Singularity

Stuttgart, 3 November 2017

I first want to say a few words about the global school and its leading faculty, the Global Event College, who are leading this 'Matrix Exploration' event in Forum-3, in which some of you are participating. The college is directing the development of the School of Spiritual Science, and its main task is to research and actualize the Christ event of our time and transform it into living community practice. The work accomplished in this School in the last decade has demonstrated that Michael's guidance can be perceived if we unite our hearts in mutual understanding, love and inspiration, and raise our perception and consciousness to the etheric world. Then he can let his forces flow into the community chalice, enrich and enhance its work, and inspire its development.

In this manner, we also demonstrate the unique harmony that comes about, when we follow Rudolf Steiner's present spiritual impulse and our free individual and social initiative. Rudolf Steiner is the herald of modern freedom and love, and he is always tirelessly trying to awaken the hearts of pupils to form a modern community of truly free people. Through many years, Rudolf Steiner has been a living partner, guide and inspirer, who stands by our work, and to follow his present spiritual work in the spiritual world is the correlative of the constant effort to become freer and more creative, human and social. The conscious collaboration with the supersensible school of Michael, described in my various books, is the outcome of our growing together, as spirit sisters and brothers, to form the etheric bridge on earth that connects the two

Michaelic communities.[2] This also demonstrates that it is possible in this century to resurrect spiritual science, founded a century ago, and that it can once again express the living spirit of the present.

Our subject in the two lectures today and tomorrow is a deeply esoteric one, called *Ahrimanic and Michaelic Immortality*. To understand why it is possible to attain these polar opposite immortalities in the present age, we must first bring before us an indication that Rudolf Steiner gave about the current transformation of the etheric body. This transformation is the release of the etheric heart from the physical heart. Rudolf Steiner said that the etheric head has been released from the physical head since ancient Greece and that the etheric heart will be fully released from the physical heart over the period 1721-2100 AD. He says that 'since the third century BC the old intimate connection between the etheric head and the physical head has been lost'. This is the reason why in Athens humans could begin to think in a free manner, not only receiving divine thoughts as inspirations from the gods. On the other hand, 'the intimate connection was still maintained between the physical heart and the etheric heart until the year 1721'. This means that from the beginning of the eighteenth century, 'the connection between the human physical and etheric heart will grow weaker, in a remarkable way and the etheric heart will be totally released from the physical heart in 2100'.[3] This fact is of the greatest importance for all the present and near future development of the real Michaelic work and also for the worst ahrimanic and luciferic possibilities, also described in *Spiritual Science in the 21st Century*. And this is the decisive indication, that 'the released etheric body will

---

[2] The efforts to actualize the archetype of the School of Spiritual Science is described in my book, *The Twilight and Resurrection of Humanity, The history of the Michaelic movement since the death of Rudolf Steiner. An Esoteric Study* (Temple Lodge 2020).
[3] Lecture of 5 April 1919 (GA 190).

acquire a right connection to the spiritual world only when humans strive for spiritual knowledge'.[4]

This development made it possible to describe in my book, *Cognitive Yoga: Making Yourself a New Etheric Body and Individuality*, how the etheric body is separated and spiritualized, from head to heart and limbs.[5] This process starts with the spiritualization of thinking and sense-perception in the nerve-sense system in the head and is then moved via the larynx to the spiritualized forces of the rhythmic system in the etheric heart and lungs in the chest, and finally anchored in the spiritualized etheric forces of the metabolic-limb and reproductive system in the lower body. This is an individual actualization of the development of the stream of Michael during the three centuries of his present age. In the first Michaelic century, the twentieth century, anthroposophy could be grasped with the forces of the head. This gave it the common intellectual signature. In the second century of Michael, the twenty-first century, it must be consciously embodied in the released etheric forces of the heart; and in the third and last full Michaelic century, the twenty-second century, this process should be embodied in the released etheric forces of the metabolic-limb and reproductive systems.[6]

In this way, *Cognitive Yoga* described the outline, in so far as the etheric body is concerned, of what must be attained in three centuries of the present age of Michael. In the twenty-second century, the third and last full century of the age of Michael, after the etheric head and heart have been fully released and spiritualized in the twentieth and twenty-first centuries, the etheric body will have to be released and spiritualized in the

---

[4] Ibid.
[5] Yeshayahu Ben-Aharon, *Cognitive Yoga: Making Yourself a New Etheric Body and Individuality* (Temple Lodge 2016).
[6] The consequences of the release of the etheric heart for the whole human constitution, is described in the third chapter of *The New Experience of the Supersensible*, entitled 'The Evolution of Freedom'.

metabolic-limb and reproductive systems as well. In *Cognitive Yoga*, I described this process not in theoretical and general anthroposophical concepts, but as it is actualized in the real meditative praxis, step by step, in the head, heart, and the metabolic-limb and reproductive systems. In the course of this century, until the etheric heart is fully released in 2100, we must also consciously spiritualize the etheric body in the metabolic and limb system. This will prepare for its natural release in the twenty-second century and will integrate it consciously with the creative Michael-Christ forces in the etheric world, about which we shall speak tomorrow.

I have investigated the development of ahrimanic and Michaelic immortality for many years, since I realized that not only Michaelic beings are interested in the free etheric body released from the heart. The more it is released, and today most of it is already released, the luciferic and ahrimanic beings are very eager to use this opportunity to take hold of it and manipulate it for their opposing aims. They know that they have the greatest opportunity in this age to control the whole human being, because if you control the etheric head and heart, you will also control the metabolic-limb and reproductive etheric forces, and this means the whole human constitution.

So, if we fill our empty heads and hearts with dead anthroposophical concepts, and not with creative spiritual activity, wisdom and love, we offer Lucifer and Ahriman our heads and hearts, and later also our etheric limbs, as an empty space to fill and dominate. They are presently awfully busy doing this. In one lecture it will not be possible to describe how Lucifer is fulfilling his part, and we shall concentrate primarily on the ahrimanic influence.

Now Ahriman was extremely happy and enthusiastic about his great victory over humanity in the twentieth century, and couldn't stop himself from celebrating it at the end of the century in so many repugnant ways. Among so many celebrated scientific, artistic and social achievements, you will also find the globally influential inspiration, actualized at the very end of the last century, when he wrote, composed and directed the film trilogy, *The Matrix*. In these films you find remarkable luciferically coloured, ahrimanic Imaginations, staging his accomplishments in the twentieth century and celebrating their culmination at the end of the century. He also used this culmination to demonstrate his long-term evolutionary goals, showing in detail where he intends to lead us. It is extraordinarily important that at least a few people will be awakened to recognize these signs of our times in the real time of their happening and also to make it into a part of their daily practical, spiritual and social life. Let's listen carefully to the words Rudolf Steiner spoke a century ago, as he described the ahrimanic immortality project attained in the last century.[7]

I will share with you some deeply moving, indeed shocking knowledge from what Rudolf Steiner gave a century ago. While I am quoting from his words, we shall strive not merely to reflect on the conceptual contents and let our feelings echo them, but above all to kindle intensively the inner fire of enthusiasm in our hearts. We must grasp each word, each concept, with the fire burning in our free etheric hearts, igniting the courageous forces of the active will, calling us to join the creative working of the living spirit, present and active here and now, as we speak and listen.

To begin with, Ahriman strives to materialize all aspects of daily life and thus make the life after death and the life in the physical world as similar to one another as possible. This is 'the ideal of making life here on earth and life after death

---

[7] In the two lectures in Stuttgart 2017, I focused mainly on the role of Ahriman in our time. In the three lectures in Überlingen in 2022, I described the role of the two apocalyptic Beasts. In the greatly expanded new edition of *The New Experience of the Supersensible*, retitled *The Modern Christ Experience and The Knowledge Drama of the Second Coming*, the new intervention of the Asuras in human evolution is described.

similar to one another'.[8] His goal is that people will no longer experience any real difference between the life in the physical world and life after death. This is apparent, naturally, today in all aspects of life, as a result of the twentieth century. His goal is to cause more and more human souls, from birth to death, to live and die without having any spiritual thoughts, feelings and will forces. The result is that when they enter the spiritual world through the portal of death, they are totally helpless, blind and deaf and Ahriman can use them to serve his goals. Because one can only see, experience and know the life after death in the spiritual world to the extent that one has already touched the spirit during physical life. And these souls must therefore remain bound to the only form of life and consciousness they knew in physical life. This causes them to remain bound after death to the life on earth, not even realizing that they are dead.

This is the most general ahrimanic transformation of the greatest number of human souls since the end of the nineteenth century, when materialism started to take over Western civilization. In this way, human souls on the earth lose any connection to the real spirit during life and after death, and the continuity between life in the physical world and the life after death is established.

The next element in the project of ahrimanic immortality, is realized through the highly effective method for accomplishing this ideal. This is attained through the development of infinitely powerful artificial intelligence and virtual technology, such as that which is growing more powerful each day. Ray Kurzweil predicted that by 2045 the 'singularity' will be attained, which will enable the full immersion of the human body, mind and consciousness in virtual reality.[9] This means that the singularity will be complete only 55 years before the

---

[8] Lecture of 9 July 1918 (GA 181).
[9] Ray Kurzweil: *The Singularity Is Near. When Humans Transcend Biology* (Penguin 2005).

complete release of the etheric body from the heart. This is significant. This is a gigantic, world-changing, ahrimanic strategy, because if you are immersed in virtual reality most of your earthly life, you will certainly not feel that death makes any difference, because the *virtual* life simulates the life outside the body so perfectly. If it has become your true life in the physical world, then after death, you will continue to live in the same web of artificial and virtual ahrimanic intelligence. The difference is, however, that after death you are immersed directly and irrevocably, in the subhuman and subnatural ahrimanic world. You become one of its beings, and must serve its goals. And this is, for the human soul, the beginning of the fearful experience of what is called 'the second death', the death of the soul, that follows the death of the body.

This means, that we must understand the significance of the technological singularity from the anthroposophical perspective. Naturally, about this subject one could also give an entire lecture cycle. But we must say that if Ray Kurzweil is right, by 2045 millions of human beings will be embodied in body, soul and spirit, with their entire constitution, in the bodiless experience of virtual reality. Not primitive virtual headsets and virtual games, but full daily immersion in bodiless virtual reality. For the people living in this reality from early childhood as their 'natural' reality, death will not really make a difference. They will die and remain in the same virtual ahrimanic sphere of influence and experience.

From a practical point of view, we are immersed in virtual reality to begin with through our brains, the centre of the nerve-sense system. Rudolf Steiner pointed out that this is done through the forces of death in the body, centred in the brain, in which the death forces predominate over the life and building forces. These death forces are closely connected with the forces of electricity, magnetism and many other still unknown, subtle sub-sensible forces. Rudolf Steiner indicated that, 'These forces of dying away, will become more and more powerful.

The bond will be established between these forces dying within man, which are related to the electric, magnetic forces, and the outer mechanical forces. Man will to a certain extent become his intentions, he will be able to direct his thoughts into the mechanical forces.'[10] By 2045, says Kurzweil, not only our brains, but our whole body, feelings and sensations, desires and drives, will merge with this reality. This means a major transformation of the whole human constitution. Because not only the death forces of the head will be connected with this virtual world, but also the empty etheric forces released from the physical heart. And in the twenty-second century, the metabolic-limb and sexual forces will also be submerged in this ahrimanic world, in what will become an ultimate merger of the whole human body, soul and mind, with infinitely powerful artificial intelligence and machines.

We must feel it with the forces of our heart, with our spiritual will forces, not merely think about it in our abstract knowledge; we must penetrate each anthroposophical concept with powerful forces of human devotion to truth, love and creativity, *we must embody in our bodies each concept*, because if we don't take it in consciously into our released etheric heads and hearts, we will continue to offer our spiritual knowledge to Ahriman, while we are convincing ourselves, naturally, that we are serving Michael, Christ and whatnot.

The next element in the ahrimanic immortality project is based on the successful implementation of the previous elements, the all-transforming materialistic formation of human life as a whole, and the growing invasive-immersive connection to intelligent machines. Now this ahrimanic achievement has a naturally lasting effect on the increasingly free but empty etheric body. When we go to sleep at night and the astral body and ego leave the physical and etheric bodies—in the etheric body we leave behind in bed—the impact of our

---

[10] Lecture of 25 November 1917 (GA 178).

materialistic lives, thoughts, feelings, impulses and desires is accumulated. The etheric body is the body of memory; it takes in and preserves our experiences, thoughts, feeling and will impulses, desires, longings and moods. The materialistic formation of life, becoming all-pervasive and penetrating, takes over the etheric body and fills it entirely. To this etheric body the ahrimanic spirits have direct access during sleep because they filled it during the day, when our astral body and ego were inside the body, in the so-called 'waking' hours. Now in sleep, when the astral body and ego are outside, the etheric body is fully exposed to their forces, because even the slight protection that the astral body and ego provide during the day is gone, and they make the best use of this exposure.

If you saturate your soul and bodies with living and embodied spiritual knowledge, active, creative spiritual wisdom and good deeds during the wakeful hours, in the night the good spiritual beings perceive what lives and weaves in your physical and etheric bodies and let their forces stream into them, to rejuvenate them, heal them, make them fresh and creative for the next day. But to the extent that we do not nourish our daily soul life and etheric bodies with spiritual forces and substance, and instead fill it only with materialistic forces, in sleep the etheric body will be all the more hungry for the same ahrimanic substances. It will develop intense craving for this ahrimanic content and attract to itself the same forces from the lower ahrimanic etheric and elemental worlds. This allows the ahrimanic beings, 'from the earth's ether to actually give people an ether body in every state of sleep... to surround and penetrate it with an ether body from the earth's ether... Man would be able to maintain himself in his ether body, and an ethereal human race would gradually develop.'[11]

During the night, therefore, the ahrimanic forces perform a remarkable etheric transplantation. They replace the etheric

---

[11] Lecture of 3 December 1922 (GA 219).

body, which is already materialized and emptied of its original divine substances and forces during materialistic daily life, with their ahrimanic etheric body. They prepare—in their own workshops—special etheric forces and substances and plant them into our etheric body, and actually tear away our etheric body piece after piece, night after night, and gradually replace our original etheric body with their ahrimanic etheric body. A true nightmare, you would rightly say, is perceived here, when we grasp even only a glimpse of this work in our body and in the bodies of other human beings. It is indeed a painful and disturbing experience that one must undergo in this field of esoteric investigation.[12]

When the first conditions are fulfilled: the transforming of life as a whole, the immersion in artificial intelligence and machines, and the replacement of the etheric body during sleep, the human being is ready to enter into the state of ahrimanic immortality after death. Let us review its significance in human evolution.

As we saw, in alarmingly increasing numbers of people around the earth, the original etheric body has been emptied of its life-giving forces and filled to the brim with materialistic thoughts, feelings and impulses. It has become well prepared for the above-described transplantation of ahrimanic etheric forces during the night. When this transplantation has advanced far enough, this ahrimanized etheric body doesn't dissolve in the cosmic ether after death, as was the normal tendency of etheric bodies after death until recently. But what was still rather common a hundred years ago is disappearing very fast. Think about it, dear friends, how many people

---

[12] The perception and confrontation with this ahrimanic world and deeds, is described in the second volume of the new edition of *The New Experience of the Supersensible*, titled *The Modern Christ Experience and the Knowledge Drama of the Second Coming,* as part of the construction of the first etheric-cognitive layer of the bridge of spiritual memory and continuity of consciousness.

live on earth today in a thoroughly materialistic life, which means, naturally, not only in their abstract thoughts, but as the content of their feelings and especially of their will impulses. What used to be the normal development is that during the first three days after death the etheric body dissolved itself in the cosmos and the astral body and ego continued into the astral and then to the spiritual worlds. Then man went through purification in the astral world in Kamaloka, reviewed his life backwards, gathered the forces he needed to transform and correct himself in the next incarnation, and then ascended to the spiritual world to form the karma and bodies for his next earthly life. This is how it used to be a century ago!

If the astral body and ego remain bound to the ahrimanized etheric body, which stays intact after death, the human soul cannot continue to the astral and spiritual worlds and cannot form its next earthly life. This is what Rudolf Steiner called *Ahrimanische Unsterblichkeit*. It means that the soul and spirit remain bound to the materialized etheric body that never leaves the physical world after death and its life is severed from the astral and spiritual worlds and from the divinely ordained stream of karma.

However, in order to realize the full impact of ahrimanic immortality, another step on this path must be accomplished. Its significance will become clear, if we realize that not only external ahrimanic forces act on us during earthly lives, and transform our etheric body, but more importantly, an inner ahrimanic being actually lives in us, working in and on us from within. It is precisely the working of the death forces of external civilization that impact man from outside, and the inner ahrimanic being from inside, which brings about the full actualization of the project of ahrimanic immortality.

Therefore, we must enter more deeply into some of the secrets of the human constitution in the present age. In the present age, when we incarnate in the physical body, our soul cannot fill it as was possible in previous times. The reason is that our physical body has become much harder and as we saw above, the etheric body is gradually withdrawing from the physical body. This is a natural death process. Humanity and the earth grow older, and this gradual dying will continue until the physical death of the earth is complete. But we accelerate this natural death process, which has its divinely ordained time schedule and rhythm, by giving in to the above-described ahrimanic influences. Now into the bodily gap that we cannot fill with our living soul, which opens up before birth—more precisely before conception— an ahrimanic being creeps in. This must happen in our time in order to pull us deeper into physical life in the material world, in this age of the consciousness soul, the soul member most strongly connected to the physical body. Each one of us received before birth an individualized ahrimanic being into the deep unconscious regions of our soul and bodies. This is something that we must go through in this time, and this being makes us even more wide awake and clever, intelligent, in all things materialistic and subhuman. Rudolf Steiner called it the *ahrimanic Doppelgänger*, in his lecture about 'geographic medicine' delivered in St Gallen on 16 November, 1917.[13] We can briefly address only those aspects of the rich contents of this lecture, which add important knowledge to the subject of ahrimanic immortality.

For our subject tonight, the most important part of this knowledge is that the ahrimanic Doppelgänger that enters into us at birth, has a strong desire to also die with us, remain united with our soul when we die, in order to enter with us into the spiritual world when we pass through the portal of death. As an elemental-etheric being, he most ardently desires to unite with our soul so strongly, and enter with us into the spiritual world, which he can only do if he remains united with us when we die. This is indeed a remarkably interesting

---

[13] GA 178.

fact, which comes up very intensely into the light of Imaginative perception, the more we familiarize ourselves with the forces of death in general and with the forces of the ahrimanic Doppelgänger in particular.

Now, on 16 November 1917, Rudolf Steiner says that so far the ahrimanic Doppelgänger has not been able to fulfil his desire. It must be understood that ahrimanic beings are elemental beings living in the etheric and elemental worlds closest to the physical world, and don't have a soul and spirit as humans have. But they long to have them, and they can only acquire them if they take them from an ensouled and spiritual being. The Doppelgänger would attain this if he could be so strongly united with the human soul during life and sleep, that it would remain united with the soul after the human crossed the threshold of death and could enter with man into the spiritual world. Above all, as we showed, to achieve this it is necessary that such a soul has been fully transformed through a completely materialistic life. This is therefore the precondition to allow the Doppelgänger to remain united with the human soul after death. And because this human soul remains bound to earth after death, chained to its ahrimanized etheric body, the ahrimanic being will be able to possess it after death as he did in earthly life. The ahrimanization of the soul during physical life would in this way be wholly merged with the ahrimanized forces after death, and the strongest ahrimanic bonds would unite man's life on earth and after death and enslave it to its subhuman etheric and elemental worlds.

In the past the ahrimanic Doppelgänger was forced to leave the body three days before death, and with the forces of ancient clairvoyance, people could still experience this in various ways. People could experience this being departing and therefore know that they would soon die. Thus, the last three days could be experienced as special days, often with heightened consciousness, and they could gather family and friends around their bed, heal some family wounds, bring order to unfinished relations, and then depart peacefully. The modern souls who succumb to the ahrimanization of all aspects of life, have long lost this atavistic experience, but on the other, ascending path of our evolution, when the new soul faculties begin to evolve through the meeting with the etheric Christ available since the end of last century, this experience will emerge in a new and conscious form.

Now we have a fuller picture of what ahrimanic immortality really means. These souls are bound and enslaved to the ahrimanic forces of the earth before and after death and have forgotten their true soul and spirit nature, their karma and repeated earthly lives, and their connection to the true goals of human evolution. They do not wish to be born again to continue to develop themselves and humanity, and when you try to tell them about it, they react as materialistic people do, with great antipathy and repulsion.

The main goals of Ahriman described thus far are summarized by Rudolf Steiner in this way:

> The object is this: through a certain schooling, a certain acquisition of forces, to transpose certain human souls into a condition in which, after death, they feel themselves more and more akin to the conditions and forces of the earth, acquiring almost a mania for the earth-forces—of course those of a spiritual nature—quitting the neighbourhood of the earth as little as possible, remaining in close proximity to it, and by means of this nearness hoping to live on as 'the souls of the dead' around the earth, exempt from the necessity of again entering physical bodies. The Anglo-American element is striving after a remarkable and strange ideal: no longer to return into earthly bodies, but through the souls of the living to have an ever-greater influence on the earth, becoming, as souls, more and more earthly. All efforts are thus to be directed to the ideal of making life here on earth and life after death similar to one another. This will be attained—in our day only by those instructed according to this rule, which will become more and

Ahrimanic Immortality, the Matrix and Technological Singularity 17

more the prevailing custom—as an immeasurably greater, stronger attachment to the earth than the recognized 'normal' one.[14]

Now, after sharing this grim picture, Rudolf Steiner also offered some good news for half of our listeners, saying that this ahrimanic ideal can be actualized only through the male and not the female body, and further that above all in America, where the forces of the ahrimanic Doppelgänger are especially strong, true social and political progress can only be achieved through women!

We enter more deeply into the mysteries of the ahrimanic Doppelgänger, if we realize the cause of its greatest desire to remain united with us when we die. It wants to—paradoxically —'conquer death' through us. This is truly a contradictory terminology, but it must be used if we want to understand the deeper meaning of ahrimanic immortality. This actually means that the Doppelgänger becomes immortal together with the soul which it possesses. Through the Doppelgänger, the human soul attains ahrimanic immortality, the reverse of spiritual immortality. This is attained with its transmuted, ahrimanized bodily and soul forces, and at the same time, the Doppelgänger, which is an etheric-elemental being, attains through the human soul an experience of soul and spirit. It experiences for the first time what it means to possess soul and spirit, of course in a fully ahrimanized way, as its *soul-spiritual* immortality. A remarkable demonic essence exchange takes place in this manner, in which the human soul is degraded to the etheric level of the subhuman ahrimanic world, and the ahrimanic being sucks in, vampire like, the forces of the

---

[14] Lecture of 9 July 1918 (GA 181). The perception and confrontation with this ahrimanic world and deeds, are described in the second volume of the new edition of *The New Experience of the Supersensible*, titled *The Modern Christ Experience and the Knowledge Drama of the Second Coming*, as part of the construction of the first etheric-cognitive layer of the bridge of spiritual memory and continuity of consciousness.

human soul and transmutes them with its ahrimanic soul forces. What is more, the human soul will experience the Doppelgänger as its new 'I', as indeed it already experienced it on earth, and the Doppelgänger will experience the human 'I' that it now fully possesses, as its own new soul-spiritual 'I'. In this reversed essence exchange, the human soul becomes ahrimanized and the ahrimanic beings become ensouled and spiritualized, and a new ghost-like, zombie race is created, composed of ahrimanized human souls merged with ahrimanic beings.

This was the great future ideal of Ahriman at the beginning of last century, and after Rudolf Steiner and anthroposophy left the earth in 1925, nothing could have prevented him from actualizing it ever since the 1930s and 40s up through the end of the century. And at the end of the century Ahriman could be, in his frivolous way, uproariously happy, celebrating his victory in all fields of life, knowledge, culture and society. As Rudolf Steiner said in 1924, Ahriman's role as a brilliant author, writing the last books of Nietzsche, is just the beginning of his coming performances. I am certain you won't believe that Ahriman lags behind himself and remains a mere author, limiting himself to the ancient art of book writing! Oh no, technology is his thing, and he creates and uses all the newest media to influence as many people as possible. He definitely moves on with the technology that he inspires! Therefore, as we mentioned at the beginning of the lecture, it is fitting that for his celebrations at the end of the century, the end of the second millennium after Christ and the victorious entry into the third millennium, he would choose the film medium, to demonstrate his present and future capacities and vision. One such celebration among so many, was expressed through the Matrix film trilogy released right on time: *The Matrix* in 1999, and *The Matrix Reloaded* and *The Matrix Revolutions* in 2003. Between them, right in the middle, falls the planned destruction of the Twin Towers in New York on 11 September, 2001. Let us briefly look again into some aspects of this modern myth created by Ahriman.

Those of you who are participating in the College event this week would have experienced what is so remarkable about this trilogy, because it demonstrates how far the project of ahrimanic immortality progressed in the twentieth century, thanks to the suppression of the etheric Christ impulse. This can be seen if we realize how Ahriman appropriated and reversed the old and the new spiritual traditions and symbols of humanity, and also the new revelation of the etheric Christ, and used them for this purpose. We can also say that brother Lucifer joined gladly in the celebrations of the century's culmination, leading many spiritually inclined people to Ahriman, who eagerly embraced this reversal. Only search for a moment on the Internet for all of the fantastic spiritual interpretations of *The Matrix*!

Let me just point to the final scenes of the last film of the trilogy, *The Matrix Revolutions*. Recall how Neo's sacrifice is portrayed, as he merges with the machines to save Zion, dies into it and is resurrected, like Christ. Recall how this is filmed, with all the lights, colours, and words taken from the spiritual traditions of salvation! And if you didn't fall into the luciferic trap of believing that this is a true spiritual happening—Lucifer is always ready to create a colourful aura of light around Ahriman's machines—adapting the naïve and romantic spiritual interpretation of *The Matrix*, you will have realized that in fact Neo was a more advanced instrument manufactured by the machines, to tear and appropriate from the human soul new ideals and forces that were not accessible to Ahriman before, and to transmute them into ahrimanic forces. Then you see with what ahrimanic acumen and brilliance this is accomplished, to create a new and deeper cycle of programming of the Matrix, in which through the stronger enslavement of humanity, deeper soul forces would be reversed and transmuted than in the previous Matrix cycle. Ahriman portrays this as the most exact reversal of what the true meaning of the etheric Second Coming could have been if humanity had united consciously in the twentieth century with the etheric Christ and not with infinitely intelligent machines.

Consider the fact that Ahriman could appropriate so many millions of human souls and reverse the highest ideals of humanity by the end of the twentieth century. When you admit this ahrimanic victory, you must at a certain point ask yourself, justifiably: Has there been a reappearance of the etheric Christ in the twentieth century? You may even begin to doubt if it actually took place at all, because when you survey the entire anthroposophical literature on the subject you will find absolutely nothing! People simply repeat what Rudolf Steiner said about it a century ago, and staunchly ignore what we have been communicating about it since 1993. If your connection to modern spiritual science is honest and earnest, and you consider this fact, you must be deeply moved, indeed, you must feel that your whole spiritual situation in the world is hanging on a cliff over an abyss. If this is the case, you would prepare your souls and hearts, to enter even more deeply into the Christ mysteries of our time. And then you will realize that the attainment of this ahrimanic immortality is not yet the whole picture, it is also a step leading to a more comprehensive ahrimanic goal. But nowhere is the gap between what we *know* and what we *are* as great and deep as in this field. The experience of this gap and abyss must become an existential situation if our striving is true; and it must lead us to search ever more deeply into the mysteries of our individual and universal-human being and becoming in the apocalyptic age of Michael.

If you listened to Rudolf Steiner's words about ahrimanic immortality cited above in a more inward way, you could experience this as shattering knowledge. If you are hearing it for the first time and you are not shocked, kindly talk about it with your therapist. And if you hear it a second, third, or tenth time and your heart and soul, and above all, your active and creative will is not wholly transformed and activated, go to your parish priest, because your therapist can no longer help you! This knowledge must be experienced as deeply shattering, in the deeper regions of the soul, in which we are connected to the destiny and fate of humanity and the earth, sliding so fast into the abyss of the grave of civilization. We must ask ourselves: If it is true that millions and millions of our brothers and sisters are already part of this army of the earthbound dead souls, where is the living, active, redeeming activity of the etheric Christ, whose reappearance Rudolf Steiner predicted would begin in the 1930s?

To answer this unsettling question, we must probe more deeply into our subject matter.

Thus far, we have described how ahrimanic immortality applies to individual human souls. But those human souls, beside the many ill-fated services they are obliged to render to the ahrimanic beings, must also serve Ahriman's higher and universal goal, which is to suppress Christ's appearance in the etheric world ever since 1933 and take His place. Of course, if since the 1930s and 40s people would have perceived the etheric Christ, walking among them through the twentieth century, the whole project of ahrimanic immortality would have been neutralized significantly. That is, to secure ahrimanic immortality for *humanity as a whole*, collectively speaking, the etheric Christ must not be perceived and understood, and no knowledge about His etheric being and appearance should be allowed to enter human consciousness and life from the twentieth century onward.

Rudolf Steiner spoke about this on 18 November, 1917, two days after the lecture in St Gallen about the Doppelgänger and while the final stages of the Bolshevik Revolution were taking place in Russia, almost 100 years ago to the day:

> These occult brotherhoods... have the desire to take over the sphere of influence created by Christ in the twentieth century and

in the future... and to replace him with another individuality that did not even appear in the flesh at some point, but is only an ethereal individuality, but a strictly ahrimanic nature.[15]

Speaking as we do out of occult duty and not from any personal desire, we must say today—after a whole 3x33 year cycle has been completed since Rudolf Steiner said these words—that what in his time was still only optional and in preparations, has now been fulfilled in the course of the twentieth century. In the future, it will hopefully be possible to speak in greater detail about how this process developed through the twentieth century and how up to the end of the century the reappearance of the etheric Christ was suppressed and replaced by the strictly ahrimanic being. For now, we must limit ourselves to a few aspects only.

Just consider how, with such a cynical grin, Ahriman celebrated the tremendous cleverness of his victory in 1999-2003, about how incredibly brilliant and globally influential was his performance. But why was it so effective? Its power is based on his ability to fully *reverse* the spiritual task of the twentieth century. Until the end of the century, Ahriman had indeed succeeded in suppressing the new Christ impulse and subjugated many millions of souls to ahrimanic immortality. And at the end of the century, he could still believe that he could justifiably declare, 'I have taken Christ's place and humanity has lost the Christ entirely'! Usurping the sacred spiritual traditions of sacrifice, love, and resurrection, and appropriating them to his goals, he could merge humanity with his forces, instead of with the forces of the etheric Christ. In *The Matrix* you can experience, through the power of film-making, the culmination of what he accomplished in the grave of civilization on all levels: the far reaching ahrimanic-luciferic reversal and transmutation of humanity, which took place through the whole twentieth century, ending in this ahrimanic culmination

---

[15] Lecture of 18 November 1917 (GA 178).

and victory, after he replaced the etheric Christ with a powerful ahrimanic being and enshrined him in the holy of holies in the temple of the human soul and the earth.

Dear friends, so far it could seem that I have only offered you bad news, namely, that what Rudolf Steiner warned us about, everything that he hoped would not be fulfilled in the twentieth century, has been realized. However, the fact that this knowledge can be communicated today means that Ahriman's victory at the end of last century was not as complete as he would have imagined. Despite his declarations and celebrations of global victory, it was possible, ever since the end of the twentieth century, to experience, investigate and communicate the timely results of current spiritual scientific investigation. But this means a real victory over Ahriman! Only the new Christ impulse, illuminated by the present inspiration of Michael, can make this happen. The knowledge I communicated above, and also in my books since the 90s of last century, must have been extricated from Ahriman's claws through great efforts. He did everything he could so that his victories would remain hidden and unknown, and that humans would continue to worship him as the new Christ and saviour. The knowledge that exposes his being and activities and places him in the centre of the bright light of new spiritual knowledge is what he fears most and therefore constitutes the first part of the good news, the second part of which we will add tomorrow.

This knowledge is gained thanks to the currently living and active forces of spiritual science, available through the new impulse of Michael. And the very fact that such spiritual knowledge has been available on earth since the end of the twentieth century, is the proof that Ahriman was too eager, too rushed in his desire to declare total victory. At one point, even if, quantitatively-physically speaking, ever so small, his absolute domination was broken through, and a spiritual hole was punched through his overarching global dome. Because if what Ahriman wanted us to believe at the end of last century was the only truth, that his victory was total victory, we could not stand here and communicate this spiritual knowledge. We could not have resurrected the spiritual science, which Rudolf Steiner gave a century ago, and connect it with the new Michaelic stream that has been flowing to earth since the end of last century, and unite the two, to create the new Michaelic movement in the twenty-first century.

These communications can kindle in our free etheric hearts the flame of courage to face the truth about last century, which even today, in 2017, only very few people dare to face. This flame is the only fire that Ahriman fears and cannot subjugate. But the first revelation of the spiritual truth is sombre; it demands courage to accept it, and it means that we must update what Rudolf Steiner said about the choice humanity would confront at the end of the twentieth century. In 1924 he said that, 'Humanity stands today before a great alternative: it can either watch all that is civilization fall into the abyss, or it can raise it up through spirituality, can take it further in the spirit of what lies in the Michael-impulse, which stands before the Christ impulse.'[16] And elsewhere he added that, 'If the decision is positive, progress will be possible; if not, the doom of the West is sealed, and in the wake of dire catastrophes the further evolution of humanity will take a course undreamed of today.'[17] We must have the courage to see the light that shines through this darkness of the twentieth century, and let our hearts respond creatively to its forces. If we do so, the twilight of humanity will be transformed into the resurrection of humanity. But in no other way will this be possible.

Speaking about World War I, Rudolf Steiner said that, 'It is difficult to find words of human language that can give

---

[16] Lecture of 27 August 1924 (GA 240).
[17] Lecture of 24 November 1921 (GA 209).

any adequate idea of the awful catastrophes...What went on between the years 1914 and 1918 was a kind of madness... Europe is bound to come to grief if attention is not turned to the spiritual foundations of human life... helping humanity to emerge from the chaos of anti-spirituality.'[18] Now if what took place in 1914-1918 was a kind of madness, which, as Rudolf Steiner says, can hardly be expressed in words, how can we find words to describe what took place in 1933-1945? What words, what language, can be used to express this situation at all?

However, as the soul of Helmuth von Moltke communicated through Rudolf Steiner in January 1924, this emergence from anti-spirituality could only be achieved at the end of the twentieth century, when for the first time Michael could find in the astral world, the path that leads to the altar, on which the fire burns that Ahriman fears. But Michael can find this altar and fire in human hearts only if by the etheric hearts, the etheric Christ is perceived. And in the free etheric human heart the decisive spiritual battles between Michael and Ahriman will be decided in the present apocalyptic age of Michael.

Dear friends, paradoxically, the good news we are going to share today is that since the end of the last century, as I described in my book, *The Three Meetings*, Michael could indeed find the path to the altar of the human heart, in which the fire of Christ is burning, and the new spiritual light of knowledge is radiating, which Ahriman fears. And this means that, though in the Ragnarök of humanity in the last century the Second Coming of Christ could be suppressed by Ahriman, it could indeed be resurrected 'in the last minute' of the century. With its resurrection, Michael's spiritual stream could be resurrected to new life on earth at the end of the century; and this Christ-Michael deed, formerly but a tiny flame that was barely visible at the end of last century, hardly

---

[18] Ibid.

surviving in the world darkness, could still be carried over the threshold separating the twentieth and twenty-first centuries and planted safely in the soil of the twenty-first century.

We speak today exactly 3x33 years after the admonishing testimonies of Rudolf Steiner were ignored by humanity and the worst eventualities that he warned about did occur in the course of the twentieth century. In the centennial of the crucial year 1917, in which the fate of the twentieth century was decided for the worst, the time has come to say what must be said, speaking to the opened etheric eyes and ears of the etheric hearts of courageous human souls, wakeful enough to see and hear and understand the signs of the times. In November 2017, a whole century after November 1917, one can and must speak to communicate this new knowledge more openly, how it was acquired, and how it is implemented in the formation of the new movement of Michael.

In this way, the good news is connected inwardly with the bad news, because bad news, if discovered and communicated by current spiritual scientific research, is really good news. It is an expression of positive and creative Michaelic forces. The recognition of the bad events of our time can only be attained through the good forces. It is not intended for spreading more theoretical anthroposophical knowledge, but as a creative and moral step in the transformation and redemption of the bad events into a higher good. Because one can only create the good in our time if one is fully capable of seeing, recognizing and transforming the reality in which we have lived in the last 100 years. In this reality, what we call 'bad' is the reverse of the highest 'good', and both are inwardly connected, are two opposite sides of human reality. Both stem from the source of the new revelation of the life, death and resurrection of the etheric Christ, inspiring infinite love, hope and faith.

This is indeed still a narrow path that very few people are looking for, and the bridge over the abyss of Ragnarök must still be completed. In the coming years, the bridge of spiritual memory and continuity of consciousness, outlined in 1995 in *The New Experience of the Supersensible,* must be consciously constructed between earth and heaven, between the Michaelic community on earth and the school of Michael in the etheric world. And this will be our task tomorrow, to describe some aspects of this Michaelic work with the new etheric forces, 'reversing the ahrimanic reversal' of last century, doing in the twenty-first century the exact opposite of what Ahriman and his troops have been doing since the last century. But you can only actualize the goal of Michaelic immortality and construct this etheric bridge with the forces of resurrected spiritual science, connected consciously to the revelation of the etheric Christ and the new impulse of Michael.

As we shall show tomorrow, one thing above all must be inscribed most seriously in our etheric hearts: we must create from the nothingness of the grave of civilization a totally new living and ensouled sphere of life, a living and creative sphere, in which the Christ will be able to dwell in our midst. Because after His natural sphere of appearance was usurped by Ahriman in the last century, He can only appear and dwell among us in this century if we recreate this sphere out of the forces of our free etheric hearts; its formation in the true community of Michael must become a sacred, earnest, festive situation and event, which embodies His appearance, words and deeds. This can only be accomplished by our own free individual and communal work, because His proper etheric sphere in the etheric world has been taken over by Ahriman. It will be our task tomorrow, therefore, to describe some aspects of this work, arising from the recent spiritual scientific investigations and the community formation process over the past few years.

Lecture 2

Michaelic Immortality

Stuttgart, 4 November 2017

I wish to welcome the new people who have joined us tonight and also our School friends who are participating in the Matrix-Exploration event. This event about *The Matrix* has been organized by the faculty of the Global Event College, the leading group of the global School of Spiritual Science, whose main task is to research the Christ events of the twentieth and twenty-first century and to develop the tools to create the new community of Michael in our time.

To prepare the ground of our free etheric hearts for the lecture today, we can contemplate a statement of Rudolf Steiner in one of the morning discussions during the Christmas Foundation Conference. It can help us free our minds and hearts, feelings and will forces, from the burden and shackles of the past century, to realize that the true Time Spirit, Michael, is evolving positively all the time, and that we can unite with his stream and receive his inspirations, if we raise our etheric hearts to the etheric world, in the centre of which the revelation of the etheric Christ in this century is taking place.

> I have often stressed amongst us that if you want to live in reality and not in ideas, then the realities of the time must be given particular recognition. The time in which one lives is a reality. But it is difficult to generate an understanding for this time as being something real. There are still people today who represent the threefolding of the social organism with the very sentences I used to use with regard to the conditions prevailing at the time, in 1919. History is indeed advancing so rapidly just now that if someone

describes things in the way they were described in 1919 this seems to be hundreds of years out of date.[19]

This naturally applies to all aspects of the 100-year-old anthroposophy, about which people speak today in the same words that Rudolf Steiner used a century ago. Well, then, if four years were experienced by Rudolf Steiner in 1924 like hundreds of years, what would we have to say after an entire century has passed? How many thousands of years went by during the last century? And how far are we out of date? To be *updated*, in this sense, means to lift up and transform our traditional intellects, habitual minds, our norms of living and acting, that—to tell the truth—never even made it into the real time stream of the twentieth century, not to mention the twenty-first. We must plunge into the positive stream and evolution of time, the new human-earthly Sun stream of time, which since 1879 is the living body, soul and spirit of the Time Spirit, Michael, about which we shall speak today.

Yesterday we brought before us some quotations from the lectures that Rudolf Steiner gave 100 years ago about the ahrimanic plans for the twentieth century. Let me recap in a few words what we said yesterday. The ahrimanic plan has two main goals closely connected. The first is to materialize human life on earth to such an extent that when people die, they will not experience any difference between physical life and life after death. The human souls that are transformed by ever stronger materialistic influences, who pass their entire physical life without receiving any spiritual knowledge, feelings and practice, will remain after death, bound to the earth for longer periods of time, and if Ahriman achieves his ultimate goal, they will remain bound to the earth forever.

The other goal of Ahriman is to suppress the appearance of the etheric Christ in the etheric world that began in 1933. The goal of Ahriman is to ensure that the new

---

[19] Lecture of 31 December 1923 (GA 260).

Christ impulse will remain unperceived and unnoticed by humanity, and he accomplished this also with the help of the earthbound ahrimanized human souls. Rudolf Steiner pointed out in 1917 that the goal of Ahriman, is not only to suppress the reappearance of the etheric Christ, but also to usurp His sphere of life and give it over to a strong etheric ahrimanic being. The sphere of Christ's etheric appearance that has been cleared for him by Michael and his hosts since 1879, which should have helped humans to receive the Christ consciously since the 30s and 40s of the last century, would instead be ruled by Ahriman and his beings. This is the ultimate reversal of human evolution: the replacement of the etheric Christ by an etheric ahrimanic being. And we had to say that according to our spiritual investigations, Ahriman greatly succeeded in achieving these goals in the course of the last century, and he will continue to attain his goals for the twenty-first century, if there is no opposition from the Michaelic side.

But what does it really mean that Ahriman replaced the etheric Christ with one of his etheric beings? We pointed out that in *The Matrix* trilogy you could see what a great advance Ahriman made in the last century due to this reversal, demonstrated by the fact that he could appropriate and copycat the highest human ideals of love and sacrifice, and indeed, reverse the meaning of the present Christ impulse, to portray ahrimanic immortality in the guise of human salvation. He showed brilliantly how humanity merges with his infinitely clever machine intelligence instead of with the etheric Christ. And when Neo merges with the mainframe of the ahrimanic power at the end of the third film, sacrificing himself to save humanity from the Matrix, if we are naive and romantics, and our spirituality is not grounded in the true understanding of reality, we would believe that he is following the Christ, not Ahriman! This is the meaning of Ahriman's victory, replacing the Christ with his representative, and this is the deeper meaning of the project of ahrimanic immortality, accomplished with such tremendous success in the last century. This was described yesterday in connection with the further development of the ahrimanic Doppelgänger. Ahriman was actually enriched by the appropriated and reversed human forces; he developed himself and his sub-human kingdom further, because he could usurp forces of the human soul, which he could never possess before.

Until the middle of the twentieth century, Ahriman could only advance as far as controlling the human intellect, but since then he has been able to take over human feelings and will forces. He could do this because he took control of the freed forces of the etheric heart, which remained empty because the appearance of the etheric Christ was suppressed, and he filled them with ahrimanic forces. This was the real reason for Ahriman's great satisfaction and jubilation at the end of last century, since he can now control and use not only the intellect, based mainly on the etheric and physical forces, but also even the soul forces of countless human souls bound to his kingdom. Ahriman can now strengthen his enslavement of humanity to *his* earth to a far greater extent than was possible when Rudolf Steiner warned in 1917 about his plans for the twentieth century. These are not mere conjectures, dear friends, but realities that one had to confront at the end of last century, in one's struggles to break through these ahrimanic achievements, in order to bring the suppressed appearance of the etheric Christ to full consciousness, and unite once again with the present guidance of Michael.

To place these stark developments in the context of the struggles to resurrect the Michaelic stream in our time, I will share some aspects of my work since the end of the last century. I do this because in this case the personal is not only personal, but also has a universal human meaning, which each honestly striving person in our time can relate to and learn from. It will also shed some light on the subject of Michaelic immortality, as we shall see below.

At the end of the last century, I said to myself again and again: When I observe the above-described victories of Ahriman in the twentieth century, I experience some grave questions concerning the present situation of humanity. These questions filled my soul at the end of the last century. Especially the late 90s were a time of great inner struggles, because I clearly perceived that Rudolf Steiner's worst predictions for the twentieth century had been fulfilled, and that humanity and anthroposophy with it were falling ever deeper into the 'the grave of civilization' as he called the situation of humanity at the end of the century, if the Michaelic movement failed to achieve its goals. True, I could, in my own quest for spiritual knowledge, find a way at the end of the century to the new Christ revelation and I could also, to a certain extent, describe it in my first books. But facing the situation of humanity and anthroposophy I realized how difficult it was going to be to introduce the Christ impulse into human knowledge and life, when Ahriman had established his kingdom so firmly and deeply. And indeed, when I tried to introduce this knowledge through my books and lectures at the end of the century, the opposition and hostility, especially in the Anthroposophical Society and movement, was truly formidable!

You could also say that the end of the century, from 1997 until 2001, was a very lonely path. As Rudolf Steiner predicted, this was the 'time which the ahrimanic spirits wish to use most strongly...because human beings are so completely wrapped up in the intelligence that has come over them'.[20] The new light dawning from the second century of the age of Michael and the third millennium could only be

---

[20] Lecture of 4 August 1924 (GA 237).

really perceived after the turn of the century. This happened at the same time when Ahriman celebrated his victory on a global scale, heralded by the fearful destruction of the Twin Towers in New York. He was defining his new goals for the new century and millennium, in which he will also incarnate as a physical human being himself, to build and direct his spiritual school on earth. The light of the new Michaelic century appeared through the ahrimanic darkness engulfing the earth, but it remained totally hidden, while Ahriman's victories created tremendous shock waves of fear and despair around the earth. But underneath it and above it, the new light could clearly be perceived.

This narrow path had first to be created between the modern Scylla and Charybdis, the cliffs on the right and left that the path must always go through. On the one side stands the formidable opposition from those who feel that loyalty to Rudolf Steiner primarily means loyalty to his books and the cultural institutions he created. For more than a century they have been preserving the external forms, interpreting the texts, and are unaware that they are actually transforming them into impenetrable walls, which block the path that leads to a direct experience and perception of the presently active stream of Michael in the spiritual world. This is the first major obstacle on the path. And on the other hand, there are many people who desire to have spiritual visions, to indulge in wild speculations, but who shy away from real spiritual scientific work, which requires the development of new forces of thinking, feeling and will, as well as new capacities of cognition and new social faculties. Many of them flock around clairvoyant people, who exercise tremendous fascination over people today. From the beginning of my 20s, I had to struggle to create a very narrow middle path between these two vast and powerful streams, so pervasive and dominant in the Anthroposophical Society and movement as well as in the general public. To better understand the nature of this narrow middle path, and why it is often misunderstood, I would like to describe some of its salient features.

When you do real spiritual research, you strive to follow in the footsteps of the founder and pioneer of modern spiritual science, as you do in any other field of knowledge. You must really take the trouble to study and recapitulate some of Newton's and Darwin's original observations and experiments, for example, and you will not feel satisfied with second and third-hand interpretations. This is a matter of following your spiritual conscience and it depends on the honesty of your self-knowledge. Now this is a seeming contradiction that many people misunderstand: that closely following the steps of your teacher and being a free and independent thinker and scientist are two foundations of this same path. The real pioneers in all fields of science were independent thinkers, but also acknowledged the work of their predecessors, and even if they had to overcome their limitations, they first learned from their teachers' best practices and acquired their knowledge. In the modern age of the consciousness soul, in which natural and spiritual science has developed for the first time in history, you have to find your own way by means of your own forces, and to what extent you will be truthful to the path that the pioneers created, depends solely on your free cognitive and moral forces.

Now, natural scientists are hampered in their development because they completely depend on the transmitted physical traditions in their scientific fields, and because they don't follow the further development of the souls of, for example, Newton and Darwin in the spiritual world after death. But this is not the case of the aspiring pupil of spiritual science. For the spiritual scientist, the transmitted physical teachings of his teacher serve only as the means to penetrate consciously into the real spiritual world. There he strives to consciously grasp the present development and work of his teacher, who has greatly progressed since his last incarnation. You study and assimilate as seriously and deeply as you can all the transmitted spiritual knowledge given in the books of spiritual science, and all the cultural and social institutions that Rudolf Steiner created a century ago. You take it all in with outmost devotion and earnestness as you also assimilate with gratitude all the great spiritual creations of humanity through the ages. But for you the study and recapitulation of the spiritual traditions is the means to the real goal. It is the beginning of your work and not its ultimate goal.

This must be emphasized very pointedly, because in all spiritual traditions and institutions, including the Anthroposophical Society and movement, this is completely misunderstood. The study of the transmitted books and cultural creations of your teacher, preserved physically on the earth, has the same function that physical food has for your body: you know that if you want it to nourish and replenish your physical forces, you must thoroughly consume and annihilate it in the depth of your metabolism. You don't want to preserve the tomato and cabbage in your stomach! You destroy it *to extract its inner formative forces*, not to preserve its dead substances and forms. It is therefore the most elementary requirement for the true pupils of spiritual science, that they must actively assimilate, spiritualize, resurrect the old teaching and institution, release the living spiritual forces from the dead bones and shells of their past embodiments, and use them to connect to the spiritual world from which they originated. You resurrect it from the dead letters and social and cultural forms of bygone times, and it becomes a living, actual spiritual force to ascend to the spiritual world, grasp the creative, *present* spiritual source, and experience your teacher's *present* supersensible goals. The presently living spiritual teacher, not his historical-physical legacy, is your true teacher and partner, and his transmitted physical teachings must be constantly transformed to lead you to the presently active source of the true stream of Michael.

Now, if this direct connection to the spiritual teacher is established, man realizes that he is the most modern of all teachers, absolutely respecting and supporting the freedom and creative responsibility of his pupils, like no ordinary teacher does. Therefore, for example, he will never give you 'yes' or 'no' answers to your inquiries and questions. His fully modern spiritual guidance has only one goal: to help you develop your free cognitive forces, to be able to answer your questions yourself. This intercourse lifts all our mediocre concepts concerning 'freedom' and 'love' to a higher level, and gradually you become aware that this is in fact the most important teaching you receive. But there is another aspect of this spiritual teaching that is very intriguing, and it takes some time to ascertain its meaning. Let's assume that in your spiritual investigations you have attained a certain result, and you have formed some concepts to explicate it, which you may feel are quite correct.

This happens, naturally, all the time. And you may feel cautiously confident that you have achieved something valuable, and you offer it to your teacher or his spiritual companions and assistants, expecting to receive it back enriched and deepened, as has happened on other occasions. But in this case, what you experience is actually the opposite: you feel that what comes back to you—how should I put it?—is actually intended to stimulate you to confuse yourself! The result of this feedback is that what seemed to you clear yesterday becomes blurred today, certainties turn into new questions, clarities are dissolved back into conceptual chaos. The clear and formed concepts that you have created return to their creative source, and you feel encouraged to start again.

As a matter of fact, to begin with, you would want to hold on to your finished concepts and consolidated conclusions, which you are rather certain about because you invested much work in their formation, and you will incline to reject any uncertainty that clamours around it. But with time, you realize that in this manner you could also develop your cognitive forces in a very different way, to make them much more pliable, flexible and creative, and you begin to cherish this aspect of the teaching.

In other words, man has to learn to receive not only the approved reception and transformation of his offering, but often more importantly, its creative chaotization and diffusion. You must learn to accept it with creative enthusiasm, giving up the finished results of previous work and opening the soul with gratitude to the opportunity to start a new cycle of research. You learn to recognize that this gesture is a road sign placed at important junctures and turns of the path, indicating that what you have created is far from finished. 'Open it up again!', it says. 'Let its hardened shells dissolve, because you can do better. Go on experimenting and testing; do not close it too soon.' When one ventures to let it go and begins again, one is always encouraged: 'Explore further, call on the forces of creative chaos, dare to expand, make variations, use your imagination, become a listener to the inner process that works in your soul, find new expressions to describe what you will experience around the next corner, and then also try to do it in an altogether different way!'

If you overcome your pride and obstinacy, you realize that your teacher knows far better than you would ever know, what you are aiming at and what you are capable of, and he wants you to grow and become better, to improve your faculties, even if you think that you have already achieved so much. 'Give us more than the best you can produce at the moment, so we can take it up and build with it further in the cosmos and return it to you in a transformed and enriched form, as an impulse for new investigations and creations.'

This mutual dialogue and communication with the spiritual teacher and his associates in the spiritual world is the main subject of the sequel to *Cognitive Yoga*, called *Cognitive*

Yoga: How a Book is Born. Man grows with time to learn how to work with the Michaelic beings of the spiritual world and with one's teacher in such a free and creative way, which is based on trust in oneself and trust in the unshakable support and infinite wisdom of the spiritual world.

The reason why I share these aspects of my spiritual schooling, is to create a more realistic picture of what true spiritual science is, and what it means in praxis. It is important to bear this in mind, when we speak about our struggles with ahrimanic immortality, the development of Michaelic immortality, the construction of the bridge of spiritual memory and continuity of consciousness, and the formation of the new community of the School of Spiritual Science in our time.

After the ordeals at the end of the last century were over and the turn to the beginning of the new century was complete, I could feel that I had created a stable and secure bridge to the spiritual world. Now this question became the central challenge: How would it be possible, from the beginning of the twenty-first century, to use the faculties and knowledge gained in individual work, to build a community that would perform this work together, as the main task of the School of Spiritual Science? And what you realize, and this realization comes about through inner testing and probations, is that between your inner spiritual life and the people around you, a seemingly unbridgeable abyss exists. In order to live and embody this truth together with other human beings, you must develop much deeper, stronger forces of love and compassion toward yourself and your comrades. As was the case with the spiritual research in the 1980s and 90s, this task also proved more difficult than imagined.

When I observed the small band of people who had read my books and asked me to support their spiritual path and community building, I realized that beside the fact that many required faculties were missing, many obstacles were also present in the form of deeply ingrained and mistaken habits, norms and practices, which people brought from their former anthroposophical life and work. I said to myself that this situation required a somewhat radical approach. If we are truly 'to become like little children again to enter the kingdom of spiritual science', we must develop entirely new faculties and overcome deeply entrenched habits. Without this, it is absolutely unthinkable that we would be in a position as a community, to become competent in handling the art of the bridge-building, which must connect in this century the physical and spiritual worlds, the Michaelic school on earth and the school of Michael in the etheric world.

But before you can do this with others, you must do it again from the beginning, in yourself! I described some aspects of the transformation of my spiritual research in the second decade of the twenty-first century in the article, *'My Way to Cognitive Yoga'*, published in Watkins' *Mind Body Spirit* magazine.[21] To build the community of the School of Spiritual Science you must do it as a human being among humans and live this truth together with your peers. It cannot be 'taught'; it is not a matter of transmitting acquired spiritual knowledge, it is about *becoming* this teaching, growing and maturing together in a community with human beings in the present time. But this cannot be simply decided upon and accomplished in one resolution. You must *become* human in a far deeper sense than you previously thought is required and possible. But haven't you become by now an old man of 50? Have you not already consolidated your personality, habits, acquired knowledge and disciplines? And can you undo your development, to return to your fresh and innocent beginning?

To begin with, I had to intentionally recreate the original stage of consciousness from the beginning of my spiritual life. I was really striving to become in this respect 'a

---

[21] Issue: Winter, 2017.

little child again'. What was described in my book *Cognitive Yoga* came about through this process. I said to myself: Let me go back in time and place myself again in Easter 1976, reading *The Philosophy of Freedom* for the first time. In Easter 1976, this first reading led me to experience how it resonated with the experience of the etheric Christ that I had undergone exactly a year before, in Easter 1975. As I described it in *The Three Meetings*, my task in the coming decades was to bring together the results of *The Philosophy of Freedom* and the modern Christ experience, to create the fully conscious faculties of Imaginative cognition on which the Michaelic bridge is based. Now, 30 years later, I wanted to start the work with *The Philosophy of Freedom* from the very first steps of *ordinary* daily consciousness, from ordinary thinking and sense-perception, and transform it step by step into Imaginative cognition without any support from the given supersensible faculties. I suppressed all the given and acquired Imaginative faculties that I developed in the last 30 years, to perceive the sense perceptible physical world and think about it as ordinary people do. I wanted to make this process accessible to my pupils and comrades, and to demonstrate and minutely describe the path that leads from ordinary consciousness to the *first* level of supersensible consciousness. Because the formation of Imaginative consciousness is grounded in the etheric body, I described its formation from the spiritualization of the basic soul forces as organically as possible, allowing the reader to participate in the whole process with her and his ordinary thinking.

To understand this process in a deeper way, another perspective can be added. When my first two books were published in 1993 and 1995, I was aware that in the first half of my life I was supported by the forces streaming from the meeting with the etheric Christ in Easter 1975 as well as the Imaginative faculties that it awakened in my soul. I was granted the supersensible Christ experience and the Imaginative faculties that perceived it, before I met anthroposophy, and I used these forces to spiritualize the given contents and forms of physical anthroposophy and applied its spiritualized forces to my spiritual scientific research, as described in *The Three Meetings*. But now, in my 50s, I felt a real passion to reverse this process. Of course, I was working with my free human forces all along; after all, *The Philosophy of Freedom* was my first foundation. Nevertheless, the given Imaginative faculties were naturally active as well, and the outcome of the synthesis between the given supersensible faculties and the spiritual scientific work, constituted the content and form of my work in the first part of my life and my first books. This was necessary, and the work was fruitful, and had to be undertaken in this way. But towards the end of the 90s, when the forces of my consciousness soul were fully developed, and then after the turn of the millennium, when the forces of the spirit self were developing, I couldn't rest content with this accomplished work.

Also recall that what we bring with us from previous incarnations to the present life as given supersensible faculties as well as ordinary talents, belong to the domain of Lucifer. Lucifer controls all spiritual achievements from the past, as long as they are not transformed in the present. What we bring from the past and use in the first part of life, must be wholly transformed in the second part of life, to become achievements of the *present* life which means also of the epoch of the consciousness soul in which the present Christ impulse takes place. Otherwise, as so often occurs, in the second half of life Ahriman harvests the fruits of Lucifer's influence from the first half and uses them to further his goals. This is the fate of many creative people, who stop developing at the end of their 20s. But if you overcome Lucifer's heritage in the first half of life, you can also confront Ahriman in the second half of life. I was fully conscious of this during the end of the last century and the beginning of the present century. But I still had to struggle to find the way to make the transition and transformation from the first to the second halves of my life, and what I described above was the solution to this challenge. I wanted to enter the etheric world and recapitulate the original meeting with the etheric Christ, which was experienced as a given grace, and attain it as a result of my free spiritual scientific activity. And then I wanted to find the way to make it available to the faculties of those human souls who wished to join the School of Spiritual Science.

Now, as we speak in 2017, 3x33 years after the most decisive year of our last century, in which the twilight of humanity took place, what are the current and next goals of our work?

As victorious Ahriman continues his march through the first part of the twenty-first century, building his kindergarten and lower school as a preparation for his occult high school during his coming incarnation; when the technological singularity arrives in 2045, and Ahriman successfully binds millions of souls before and after death to his kingdom, where ahrimanic immortality will be celebrated, the Michaelic etheric singularity, if you want to use this expression, or the Michaelic bridge, must be completed. This means that enough people must be able to develop, before the middle of the century, the faculties to communicate in full consciousness with the supersensible school of Michael in the etheric world. A small Michaelic community, school and movement must be as vibrantly alive and creative as the ahrimanic school and movement, fired by the holy enthusiasm of Michael and the healing flames of Christ and the earth's etheric resurrection. We must place all our best forces in the service of this critically decisive task, and this is the reason why it must be consciously started in 2017, to be developed through the coming 2020s and 30s, and continued into the 2040s to attain this goal.

As we showed yesterday, ahrimanic immortality is based on the completely ahrimanized etheric body, so hardened in earthly life and during sleep that it remains intact after death and binds the soul to the ahrimanized forces of the old earth. The Michaelic immortality, on the other hand, is based on the new revelation of Christ's spiritual being and etheric body, perceived and individualized by the spiritualized forces of the etheric hearts, working in harmony in the Michaelic community. To attain this goal, we must learn very carefully and conscientiously, to create the new individual and communal etheric body, permeated and immortalized by the living presence of the etheric Christ in our midst. This etheric body is the counterpart to Ahriman's subhuman etheric sphere, which he usurped from the Christ in the last century. It can only come into being if we build it step by step, through our spiritual handwork. It can only be based on fully conscious work, guided by the current spiritual scientific research.

Let us compare, briefly, for the sake of clarity, the ahrimanic and Michaelic immortalities. As indicated in the previous lecture, the first, fundamental preparation of ahrimanic immortality is the ahrimanic transformation of all aspects of earthly life. After more than a century of materialism in thinking and acting, this goal has been largely achieved. In the course of the last century, Ahriman succeeded in realizing 'the ideal of making life here on earth and life after death similar to one another'. The Michaelic answer to this must be as actual and real, as practical and embodied as the ahrimanic accomplishment. Spiritual science must become a source of vital life in our etheric head, hearts and limbs, not a mere collection of abstract ideas in our empty heads, and passive feelings in our empty hearts, which Lucifer and Ahriman control, but rather surging, uplifting, vitalizing life forces, with healing and transformative forces active in all areas of daily life. In this way, we make life in the physical world so spiritual that during earthly life we are consciously connected to the Michaelic guidance in the etheric world, and after we pass through the portal of death, nothing essential has changed.

We continue to work in the same way from the other side and remain consciously united with our colleagues on earth. Connecting this side with the other side, there will stand the radiant, colourful etheric rainbow bridge, the Green Snake, the two-way bridge connecting the Michaelic lower school on earth with its high school in the etheric world and letting the guidance of Michael inspire the conscious and free human hearts in the Michaelic school on earth.

The second ahrimanic element was the merging with the infinitely powerful ahrimanic intelligence and the total immersion in virtual reality and machines. It is based on the death forces of the nerve-sense system. 'These forces of dying away, will become more and more powerful. The bond will be established between these forces dying within man, which are related to the electric, magnetic forces, and the outer mechanical forces. Man will to a certain extent become his intentions, he will be able to direct his thoughts into the mechanical force.' We can only confront this bodily formation and soul immersion in ahrimanic reality, if we create a fully conscious immersion in the living etheric reality, as a daily praxis, in all aspects of our cultural and social life.

No other force can counteract and overcome the ahrimanic forces that, in the near future, will create a far stronger ahrimanic immersion in his subhuman world. Holistic etherization of all aspects of our spiritual and social life must take place, which means to create real etheric connections and relations with each other, which will weave such strong bonds of love and trust between our etheric hearts, expressed in uplifting joy, enthusiasm and creative ideas, ideals and deeds, in comparison with which the most fantastic immersions in ahrimanic virtual reality will look like mere child's play. We must aspire to develop such intense life between us, that we will know from direct daily experience that our creative etheric deeds and words are so much more profound and exhilarating, true and human.

The third basis of ahrimanic immortality is created in the subhuman, subnatural, etheric world. As we described yesterday, if the etheric body is nourished during the day with only purely ahrimanic forces, it will be replaced piece by piece during sleep with etheric ahrimanic forces. The Michaelic answer to this, is the conscious work of building the new etheric body described in *Cognitive Yoga*. Then, during wakeful day work and during sleep, it will be enhanced through the etheric forces active in the etheric aura of the earth, in which Christ weaves in the planetary etheric ring of the earthly-human Sun. The new individual etheric body on which the Michaelic immortality is based, is connected to the planetary etheric ring, the new world of life forces, that is forming in our midst, as the new Heaven and new Earth. This is the most basic Michaelic task we have to accomplish today and in the near future, if we want to create the shining etheric bridge over the abyss of the last and present centuries. For this, the free etheric heart must become the most robust etheric pillar. It must be kindled with intense flames of devotion and brotherly love, reverence and gratitude to each other, actualized in the human meetings that form the heart of the new Michaelic community. We must attain a century later, what Rudolf Steiner experienced in his free etheric heart, when he said in 1924, that, 'Our heart has changed; we no longer bear the same heart in our chest. Our physical heart has grown harder, and our etheric heart, more mobile. *We must find access to our supersensible hearts.*'[22] This is an absolute requirement, because these heart forces alone can unite with the highly spiritual, living, and creative forces of the etheric Christ and receive the inspirations from the supersensible school of Michael.

All the Christ-given etheric forces, embodied in this way in our etheric hearts, are immortal life forces, and they don't

---

[22] Lecture of 20 July 1924 (GA 217a). My italics.

remain in the limits of the physical body, but stream out and connect with Christ's etheric forces, building up the etheric earth since the Mystery of Golgotha. 'Ever since that time,' says Rudolf Steiner, 'the human etheric body has held something that is not subject to death, to the death forces of the earth. And this something which does not die with the rest, and which people gradually achieve through the influence of the Christ impulse, now streams back again out into cosmic space; and in proportion to its intensity in man it generates a certain force that flows out into cosmic space. And this force will in turn create a sphere around our earth that is in the process of becoming a sun: a sort of spiritual sphere is forming around the earth, composed of the etheric bodies that have come alive. The Christ light radiates from the earth, and there is also a kind of reflection of it that encircles the earth...Beginning with this event the earth began to be creative, surrounding itself with a spiritual ring which, in turn, will in the future develop into a sort of planet circling the earth.'[23] This is the foundation of our entire etheric work and the real substance of the Michaelic immortality and the bridge of continuity of consciousness between the physical and etheric worlds. Ahriman can be overcome in the twenty-first century only if such a creative community builds the bridge of continuity of consciousness together.

The fourth and decisive element of ahrimanic immortality is that in the twentieth century, among a growing number of people, the ahrimanic Doppelgänger could fulfil its desire, to die with human souls and enter with them into the spiritual world after death. This being was able 'to conquer death and die with man and in this way enter the spiritual worlds that man enters after death'. This binds already today millions of souls to the ahrimanic world and forces them to serve his abominable goals after death. The Michaelic answer to this challenge is that more and more people will learn—in

---

[23] Lecture of 6 July 1909 (GA 112).

the first half of the twenty-first century—to individualize the new revelation of the etheric Christ, as demonstrated in *Cognitive Yoga*, and build for themselves, based on the new immortal etheric body, the new 'etheric individuality' as well, a Christ permeated 'I'; and that both the Christed etheric body and Christed 'I' that we create on earth, will remain with us as we pass through the gate of death. There we will continue to form the Michaelic community that we formed on earth and link the two communities together with strong bonds of love and reciprocal empowerment.

This means that when Ahriman boasts of his great achievements on earth and in the nearest subterranean etheric world, forcefully commanding his quickly growing ghostly zombie army of depraved souls, we can confront him and demonstrate the immortally-linked community of creative Michaelic souls, fired by Christ's creative fire, in direct living communication with Michael and his supersensible school. We must create, on a daily communal basis, such 'spiritual science [that] works from below upwards, stretches out its hands... to grasp the hands of Michael stretching down from above. It is then that the bridge can be created between man and the Gods.'[24] But the bridge cannot be built from the ordinary soul substance of mere thoughts, feelings and wishful desires; only a direct connection to the source of the presently active etheric Christ can supply the forces and materials required to construct this bridge. 'Christ offers himself as this material,' says Rudolf Steiner, and only through the Christ the 'material is given, out of which man can make a bridge'.[25]

This allows us to also counteract Ahriman's replacement of Christ with his strong ahrimanic representative. Ahriman took over Christ's natural sphere of influence in the twentieth century, and made it his own, with all the means described

---

[24] Lecture of 17 December 1922 (GA 219).
[25] Esoteric lesson of 16 December 1911 (GA 266).

above, and now we can take it back, establishing Christ's etheric kingdom on earth. This kingdom has nothing to do with Ahriman's world, based in the old and dying Earth and Heaven; it is the newly germinating etheric earthly-human Sun, the new Earth and Heaven of the New Jerusalem. Therefore, Christ's living, ensouled and spiritual sphere of life and deeds is no longer given by the spiritual world, and He remains homeless as long as humans do not create a new etheric home for Him and for us on the etheric earth. By creating a human sphere of vibrant life and love-giving forces, we lift the heavy ahrimanic stone placed over the suppressed etheric Christ in the course of the twentieth century and resurrect His consciousness and presence in our hearts and bring Him to life among us. It is the highest mission of the new Michaelic movement in the second century of Michael and this must be fulfilled with utmost devotion and spiritual scientific exactitude before the middle of the century, to enable the great, second incarnation of the Michaelic impulse towards the end of the century.

This means that as victorious Ahriman continues to strengthen his ironclad dominance over humanity, a lively Michaelic, Christ permeated human community must oppose and thwart him with the consciously created bridge of immortal life, in the first half of the twenty-first century. This will guarantee the continuous communication with the leadership of the school of Michael in the etheric world. It must become an actual, communal practical science, art and ritual of bridge construction, for which 'Christ offers himself as the material', in spiritualized human and social daily life. Up to the middle of the century, it may naturally only become a small enclave of true Michaelic civilization, but nevertheless it may also become a highly vital and potent seed of civilization, which proves strong enough to navigate the stormy waves of the first half of the century and makes the bridge ever broader and safer for a growing number of souls.

When this bridge is completed, the 'old man with the lamp' as in Goethe's Fairy Tale, *The Green Snake and the Beautiful Lily*, will be able to exclaim for the third time that 'the time is at hand!' and the temple of the new earthly-human Sun can rise and become visible, as the middle sphere, where free human hearts weave and beat together in the new community, fired by the heart forces of the new earthly-human Sun.

Of course, it will demand earnestly dedicated creative work to accomplish this, because it will not fall by itself from the etheric heavens as the manna did on the Israelites in the desert. We have to build it ourselves from the ground floor, from the very elementary foundations of spiritual science, step by step, fired by the love and enthusiasm of the new Christ impulse. Step by step we must prove to ourselves that we can create spiritual science anew from its true foundations, all the way to lofty spiritual heights. We test and prove, not in theory but in real spiritual communal praxis, that each step is actually accomplished in the most practical spiritual and social work, overcoming the most staunch residues of the 100-year legacy of a merely intellectualized anthroposophy. We must demonstrate to ourselves that a wholly practical path can be created, through mutual empowerment, trust and healing of our mortal, wounded selves. Then we will receive the greatest help from the spiritual world that was ever given to humans in the course of history.[26]

As a matter of fact, the veil that separates the physical from the spiritual world today, is thinner than ever before, and it is getting thinner all the time, because this is the main drive of the age of Michael. *Objectively* speaking, this is so. *Subjectively*, from the human side, the opposite is just as true: humans have in the last century made this veil

---

[26] In my book *The Twilight and Resurrection of Humanity*, the formation processes of the community of the School of Spiritual Science is described from various points of view. Among others, the creation of the future Michaelic 'school of love' is described in some detail.

compact and impenetrable. But this means, dear friends, that it is entirely up to us. It is placed squarely in our freedom, to break through our human-made walls and enter the etheric world through this thinnest veil... or harden it further. If we dedicate the fire and enthusiasm of our will, feeling and thinking, to break through our own fetters, we will find the greatest help coming towards us from the other side, as was never possible before in human evolution. This fact is one of the most remarkable experiences that one undergoes today when crossing the etheric threshold.

When you consciously perceive what is taking place in the closest supersensible world, linked most intimately with our physical earth and life, you will be highly amazed to realize where we truly stand. You will see that all the spiritual beings and human souls that remained loyal to Michael through the Ragnarök of the twentieth century, are eagerly standing in line waiting to come to our help. For more than a century they have been searching in all corners of the cosmos and earth for human souls who would want to communicate with them, and this search is so frustrating, because human souls have become so passive, arrogant, closed and isolated. They are searching so hard for souls who would want to start a creative dialogue with them, based on mutual fertilization and love. But most people are making themselves, by their free decisions and deeds, completely unreachable in our time! Either because they are sure that they are already doing the right thing, which is a common luciferic illusion in many spiritual streams, or because they are convinced that the fate of humanity has been decided for the worst and they withdraw into comfortable virtual and/or spiritual hideouts. This changes entirely when we develop real faith in the active power of the living spirit, based on practical, repeated experience, and not on concepts and theories. This faith can then create communal situations and events of practical love and mutual trust, healing and transformation, through which this communication will be made possible. When we actually do it, our spiritual companions begin to breathe happily again, and join our work in most creative ways. The beings who remained loyal to Michael and the Christ in the last century can only work in an atmosphere permeated with the deepest, most honest forces of freedom and love, mutual healing and trust, through which alone they can connect with us. This is the absolute precondition in the present age, and it will be the precondition in all future ages to come.

Dear friends, in one lecture I could only indicate that much. But, even if only briefly, I wanted to share some aspects of the real work that is being done on earth in the true school of Michael in the present and near future. Ahriman will continue to intensify his work: he never sleeps, nor do his servants. The bad guys are on fire; they work really intensely. But those who believe themselves to be good must have their holidays, weekends, summer vacations and long time outs! They are actually waiting for the age of retirement and say: Then we will have all the time we need to do our long neglected spiritual and social work! As Yeats observed so accurately in 1919, referring to the time of the Second Coming:

> The best lack all conviction, while the worst
> Are full of passionate intensity.

Kindly notice, dear friends, that when I read these lines, you instinctively and urgently put into operation the 'law of exception', the younger brother of the 'law of reversal', which we can learn to experience in the unconscious depths of our souls, if we practise honest self-knowledge. If you bring this instinctive reaction to consciousness, and pull yourself out of your comfortable state of thinking that 'I am naturally not the one who is meant here. I am the exception', then you will tell yourself candidly: 'Actually, no other person but me is meant here, because if I am honest, I must say that instinctively I consider myself to be part of "the best", but in truth I lack all true, fiery conviction toward the good! And my anthroposophical life and work is lukewarm at best on sunny days!' We will admit it only, however, if we practise truthful self-knowledge and place our etheric hands on our etheric hearts; of course we believe that we belong to the good people; good enough to deserve the next lazy pause and refuge, and can postpone our meditations and creative social engagement until we retire. Nor must we care too much about building the future Michaelic community. After all, didn't we already try it in our 20s, when we burned our fingers so badly in this fire, that we shall never risk trying it a second, or third, or fourth, or any more times. Even thinking about it is so terrifying and exhausting, isn't it? So, let's retreat into a longer respite!

But these retreats are not the rest that we need today. Are we really tired today? To be truly tired, is something that humans have totally forgotten. We say that we feel exhausted and develop chronic fatigue syndromes, and cannot sleep healthily today, because we no longer get healthily, creatively, tired any more, as in the good old days when we were working with our hands, and with more true creativity. When was the last time that we actually felt tired in our bones, after doing spiritual work, after making life-changing and healing social creations? Only then do you know what it means to become truly tired, creatively exhausted, and then you will also sleep well, and get up fresher and younger the next morning.

When the centenary of the Christmas Foundation Conference is commemorated in 2023, let us gather in a peaceful, deeply rested and healed, harmonious mood and feeling. Let us feel: well, now we can really start to create the future path. We can begin again from the beginning because we know a little better what it takes to build this Michaelic community, bridge and immortality, the seed of which Rudolf Steiner planted in the earth 3x33 years ago. Look at our older friends and see how younger they have grown and feel how much younger you have become in the last 10 years, thanks to our work together. And let's say, as old Bilbo did, standing on the shores of infinity, 'Here's a sight I have never seen before; I think I'm quite ready for a new adventure!' And you will feel the enthusiastic mood of expectation, to undertake this new creative venture, and feel that you are ready to start working on building this community in a totally new way. This is the first experience of Michaelic immortality, the etheric bridge of spiritual memory and continuity of consciousness, created by working with the etheric forces of our incarnated and excarnated friends and mentors, living on earth and in the etheric world.

I wish to end this lecture with the words that Rudolf Steiner spoke to his close pupil Gräfin Johanna Keyserlingk in June 1924 in Koberwitz. She told him that his efforts to actualize the new Michaelic impulse after the Christmas Foundation Conference were not accepted, understood or acted upon. This was three months before he stopped his external work and a short year before his death. And she wrote that, in response, he looked at her, acknowledging her judgment, and that for a moment he looked doubtful. Then he said, 'Indeed, you are right, humans are not ready to receive this today.' And to this acknowledgement he added a significant comment, and I experience it as vividly now as when I read it for the first time. He said: *'Aber Ahriman ist ja auch ein Teil des Christus'*—'But Ahriman is also a part of the Christ.' And while Ahriman is convinced and has also convinced most of humanity that Christ is a subordinate part of him, and that he has suppressed, bound, exiled, and replaced the Christ, we would strongly uphold and maintain the truth, that Ahriman is actually part of Christ and not the reverse. But we will be able to hold fast to this truth only if Christ's etheric resurrection is taking place in our midst. If we do so, we will experience how the suppressed and forgotten Christ is emerging, through our efforts, from the 'the dark gloomy foundations of the cosmic mysteries' and out of the 'grey spiritual depths through which humanity in its evolution is now passing', where Ahriman rules. And Christ's appearance, words and deeds, that Rudolf Steiner predicted in February 1917 for the 1930s and 40s, which were suppressed by dark Ahriman, will be resurrected to new life in the new etheric sphere created by human beings:

> If we take the trouble to learn to think the thoughts of Spiritual Science and make the mental effort necessary for an understanding of the cosmic secrets taught by Spiritual Science, then, out of the dark gloomy [*düster*] foundations of the cosmic mysteries, will come forth the figure of Christ Jesus, which will draw near to us and give us the strength and force in which we shall then live. The Christ will guide us, standing beside us as a brother, so that our hearts and souls may be strong enough to grow up to the necessary level of the tasks awaiting humanity in its further development. Let us then try to acquire Spiritual Science, not as a mere doctrine but as a language, and then wait till we can find in that language, the questions which we may venture to put to the Christ. He will answer; yes, indeed, He will answer! Plentiful indeed will be the soul-forces, the soul-strengthening, the soul-impulses, which the student will carry away with him from the grey spiritual depths through which humanity in its evolution is now passing, if he is able to receive instructions from Christ Himself; for, in the near future He will give them to those who seek.[27]

---

[27] Lecture of 6 February 1917 (GA 175).

Lecture 3

The Two Apocalyptic Beasts and the Mystery of the Wound

Überlingen, 3 November 2022

We want to experience human life with all the heights and depths in this historical time and feel that we are engaged in humanity's destiny with our whole being. We are not afraid to experience this. It is sometimes painful, sometimes difficult, but in other times it is also blessed with light and joy. And if you want to become fully human in the present age, you don't really want to experience the one without the other. Of course, many people prefer to experience one-sided pain or joy. They will admit only the pain and suffering, and the depression that comes with it, avoiding the creative joy of life. And others will allow only the joy and pleasures, without the pain, but both will have only half of the human experience today, and not the whole. What is more, this half of life, the one-sided pain and joy will not be the true pain and joy that can only be experienced if they are taken together, but will remain only their ahrimanic and luciferic caricatures. If you try to avoid the difficult and often painful path today, you will also miss the experience of the best forces of the spirit. Because the forces of the spirit are giving us the grace of pain so that we can improve ourselves, so that we can develop the forces of healing and the new moral forces that we must have in the future, to fulfil our true earthly goals.

The poet Hölderlin experienced this mystery very deeply. We could recently visit some of his beloved scenes on the Neckar in Tübingen and the tower in which he spent the second part of his life. And he wrote this in one of his poems: *'But where the danger is, the redeeming grow as well.'* *'Wo aber Gefahr ist, wächst das Rettende auch'*. He knew this from his life experience; if you enter into his biography as whole human beings and go with him through his life, you will see how he lived this in every day of his life from childhood until the end of his life, and then all the more strongly after his death.

And this is what we must develop in the present age. By the present age I mean not only the three and a half Michaelic centuries from the end of the nineteenth century to the beginning of the twenty-third century, but the whole fifth cultural epoch in which the consciousness soul develops until the middle of the fourth millennium. For the entire duration of the fifth epoch, we need this, this deeper soul mood, this holistic-human disposition and *Stimmung*.

This must be repeatedly said because this is really what is required from us, what we must require from ourselves, if we want to become humans of this time and not empty shells and masks. We must not rest under the time, nor above it, but must live directly in the middle of what is happening right here and now. How can one in any other way experience the history of the twentieth century with its horrors and salvations, if one does not take the deepest pain and bliss of healing into one's heart? In this age, also in our daily life, we must learn to experience the pain caused by evil with our human soul as a whole and find the grace and hope and the love and faith-giving power in the depths of our being. In the present age, the saving power is found only if we take into our free etheric hearts, the forces of evil and pain, and assimilate them so deeply, until we penetrate to their high spiritual source, from which alone true healing comes. It is the same in the life of the individual and the life of humanity. I may say: I want to meet the Christ, but I don't want to experience humanity's pain and illness nor my pain and illness, in order to assimilate it and transform it lovingly; I only want to meet the Christ to enjoy His glory and bliss. But if you say this, what you are actually saying is: I want to meet Lucifer, not the Christ. And we have spoken about it often in our lectures through the years and often referred to what Rudolf Steiner said: that the mystery of evil is only beginning to surface in human evolution in the present age and that from now until the far future, we will have to struggle with it and learn how to transform evil into the highest good. Because without experiencing this mystery, we cannot develop the strong moral forces, the healing capacities of the coming age of spirit self, and we will miss the meaning and destiny of becoming true humans on earth. We will not develop our deep moral forces, the forces of healing love, if we avoid evil, pain, and sickness. But through this experience of pain, we can find the source of healing and grace, joy and positive, creative transformation, and we are encouraged to grow on, and become the future healers that we would want to become.

Now, this was not yet required from us in the previous age. In the previous age the mystery of death was the central riddle that human beings had to begin to grapple with. But the mystery of evil was to a large extent hidden from the non-initiated. And people were actually warned: Don't look backward into the abyss of evil. You would be petrified; you would be paralysed. You could not take it. The power to take it was not yet in our evolution, because the Christ had not yet incarnated as a man on earth.

You know the biblical story about the wife of Lot, the brother of Abraham. When they escaped Sodom and Gomorrah, she was advised: Don't look back, because what you will see will petrify you. She looked back and became a stone. Also, Orpheus was told: Don't look back! But he did, and lost Eurydice, his clairvoyant soul forces. This of course had to be so in that age; the ancient forces of ancient clairvoyance had to die out, and death had to become a mystery.

But everything changes in the course of evolution, and today we are actually advised to do the opposite, because the time has come to develop the strong soul forces required to look into the abyss without being paralysed. The people who merely repeat today what was right in the previous age, ignore the present meaning of the Christ impulse. They deny the meaning of the Christ impulse because the Christ did not only gaze into the abyss of death and evil, but entered into it with His whole cosmic being, transformed the forces of death into the forces of eternal life and the forces of evil into the forces of loving healing.

If you recall, we described the new challenge of evil from different points of view, in the books, *The Spiritual Event of the Twentieth Century*, and *The Twilight and Resurrection of Humanity*, because this is the essence of the present Michaelic apocalypse, and of the evolution of the earth until its end and beyond.

In the recent lectures in Sweden,[28] that some of you could attend in Zoom, I read from Rudolf Steiner's last testamentary words spoken to the priests of The Christian Community, about the expected rising of the two apocalyptic Beasts in the course of the twentieth century: the first Beast in 1933, before the reappearance of the etheric Christ, and the second Beast at the end of the century in 1998. And I want us to contemplate together this profound mystery tonight, because it contains the key to the apocalypse of the age of Michael.

> The Beast will be let out. This means something for human evolution. Thus, very strong realities are pointed out, great, significant points in the evolution of mankind and the earth. In the year 1933, my dear friends, there is the possibility that the earth will perish with everything that lives on it, if there were not another, wise

---

[28] Lectures given at the annual Swedish global School of Spiritual Science meeting in Wendelsberg, October 2022.

institution, which cannot be calculated. It is therefore true that the calculations may not always be correct, if the comets have taken on other forms.[29]

We are not going to discuss presently how the rise of the Beast is connected to the appearance of the comets. I can only draw your attention that, according to Rudolf Steiner, the calculations that a comet would have collided with the earth and destroyed it in 1933, proved wrong and it didn't happen, because the wise order of the universe does not obey purely mechanical calculations. The comet was split and dispersed into meteoric showers and the ashes of the burnt meteors, with their cyanide content, rained down on earth and continues to live on in the earth, for good or ill, depending on what humans do with it.[30] But the rise of the Beast did take place, in all its destructive power, not through the comet, but through humanity. The physical destruction of the earth was avoided, through the divine guidance of the cosmos, but the possibility of the moral destruction of humanity must still be faced in all its seriousness.

Now the further important indication is that the Beast will rise up *before* the etheric Christ will be perceived by humanity in the right way:

> One must speak in the sense of the Apocalypse of John: Before humanity can grasp the etheric Christ in the right way, mankind must first meet and cope with the Beast who will rise up in 1933. That is spoken from the point of view of the Apocalypse.

Since I have been investigating this mystery for almost 50 years, I would like to present it to you. Can you make some

---

[29] Lecture of 20 September 1924 (GA 346). And the next quotation.
[30] The mystery of cyanide in the human body and earth in the apocalyptic context, is described in detail in the third volume of *The Modern Christ Experience and the Knowledge Drama of the Second Coming* (the forthcoming expanded edition of *The New Experience of the Supersensible*).

reasonable, logical and spiritual sense of this sentence that we just read? Hardly! Let us try, nevertheless, to shed some light on this mystery, because we are approaching its centennial in 2033, and we must demonstrate today how we are preparing the ground of our hearts for this coming momentous centenary.

The first problem is that the Beast will rise up *before* the etheric Christ will be perceived by human beings in the right way, and the second is that humanity must first be *fertig* (must consciously face and cope) with the Beast, *before* it can perceive the Christ in the right way. Steiner says that before the etheric Christ can be grasped by people in the right way, mankind must first cope with the encounter of the Beast that will rise up. We have to stop here and contemplate this sentence more slowly and thoroughly. *Before* the Christ appears, before human beings can grasp, perceive, and see the Christ in the right way, they have to first finish with, deal with, or cope with the meeting with the Beast. But *fertig* (to cope) here means: to be able to confront consciously, to recognize, the Beast. He says that we must cope with the encounter of the Beast that will arise. I have to ask you, therefore, what does it really mean that humanity must deal with the Beast as the precondition to perceive the Christ in the right way?

We face here two interrelated major problems: first, that it should happen *before* the etheric Christ is grasped in the right way. In other places Rudolf Steiner said more generally that the etheric appearance of the Christ will begin in the 1930s and 40s:

> The years 1933, 1935 and 1937 will be especially significant. Faculties that now are quite unusual for human beings will then manifest themselves as natural abilities. At this time great changes will take place, and Biblical prophecies will be fulfilled. Everything will be transformed for the souls who are sojourning on Earth and also for those who are no longer within the physical body.

The Two Apocalyptic Beasts and the Mystery of the Wound 61

Regardless of where they are, souls are encountering entirely new faculties. Everything is changing, but the most significant event of our time is a deep, decisive transformation in the soul faculties of man.[31]

Now in September 1924 he says that it will start in 1933, and that before it begins, the Beast must be confronted consciously. Therefore, the meaning of the term 'before' cannot refer simply to the difference of physical time because the rise of the Beast and the reappearance of the Christ take place almost instantaneously. It must have a deeper, qualitative spiritual meaning. The second question is even more confounding, because what can it mean to have to cope with the Beast consciously? How do you confront the Beast consciously at all? And only after you have confronted the Beast consciously, will you be able to meet the Christ in the right way. In the lecture cycle in June 1908 in Nuremberg about the Book of Revelation,[32] these mighty events are said to take place at the end of the evolution of the earth. But now Rudolf Steiner says it is going to happen in nine years!

As we showed recently in Sweden, in this lecture cycle on the Apocalypse in 1908, Rudolf Steiner presented the basic knowledge required for an occult interpretation of the Book of Revelation. Now, he was speaking in September 1924, and he could assume that the priests, who asked him to speak to them about it, are acquainted with the Nuremberg cycle. You may imagine their surprise when he brought the whole weight of these apocalyptic events to bear on the immediate future and the end of the twentieth century.

Let us briefly say something about the nature and mission of the two Beasts, as described in 1908. The first Beast will appear when the earth has completed its physical evolution and enters the astral world, as each person does after

---

[31] Lecture of 25 January 1910 (GA 118).
[32] GA 104.

physical death. And what does the Beast reveal? It reveals the unredeemed being of humanity, who rejected the Christ impulse and remained bereft of any connection to the Christ impulse. Think about it, that you would pass through all your incarnations on the earth and have actively and consistently rejected all the many opportunities to take in the Christ impulse. Collectively, what humanity will have become appears in the Imagination of the first Beast: our collective unredeemed human nature at the end of the evolution of the earth, after the earth has dropped its physical and etheric bodies and has become purely spiritual, that is, first as an astral being in the astral world. Then this gruesome Imagination will appear, expressing all the unredeemed lower forces of human nature, developed in the whole evolution of the earth. You can also say that this being is an expression of the unredeemed lower self, the un-Christed Lesser Guardian of humanity.

Rudolf Steiner points out that each person experiences this after he lays aside his physical and etheric bodies after death and begins the processes of purification in Kamaloka in the astral world. Then we experience our yet unredeemed lower self, with all the lower forces it contains. This is the first Beast with the seven heads and ten horns, the precise occult interpretation of which Rudolf Steiner offered in Nuremberg, but we cannot go into it now in greater detail.

Only one element from the complex nature of the Beast must be singled out, because it is important for our present subject. This riddle is indicated when the Book of Revelation says that one of the heads of the Beast appears to be mortally wounded and miraculously healed. And this healed wound gives the *second* Beast its greatest suggestive power. This is said in the language of Chapter 13 of the Book of Revelation.

I gave a first interpretation of this mystery in the second chapter of my book, *The Event in History, Science, Philosophy* and Art, 'The event in history'.³³ I briefly described one aspect of the meaning of the wound and its miraculous healing, and why it gives the second Beast such great power over humanity to realize its aims, working together with the first Beast.

So, this is the first Beast that rises from the sea, the astral world, after the final spiritualization of the earth. Now, if you imagine yourself listening to this new lecture on 20 September, 1924, you must be deeply shocked to hear that the Beast is going to rise up in nine short years, in 1933, after it was said in 1908 that it will appear in the astral world after the end of the physical evolution of the earth! Here real spiritual science begins for those 'who have eyes to see and ears to hear' the signs of the time. But we must become truly awake and alert, to experience and decipher the apocalyptic mysteries of the present age of Michael.

We can take a preliminary step towards the understanding of these mysteries if we realize, as Rudolf Steiner said many times, from different points of view, that we have passed the middle of the evolution of the earth in Atlantis and today we live closer to its end. This means that the earth is getting older and is already in a process of dying. The same happens in our individual development. We grow older as individuals over decades, and many things take place in our life that in their full form will appear at death, but nevertheless they begin to appear in the second part of our life. We constantly die, naturally, every moment after birth, but until the middle of life, the life forces are stronger than the forces of death. In the second part of life, death becomes stronger, and the forces of life recede. And long before man dies at the mature age of 70 or 80, he experiences this dying in partial forms, in moderate forms, gradually. The second part of our life and of the life of the earth is therefore apocalyptic, it is all about the revelation of the future spiritualization of everything that we call

---

³³ *The Event in Science, History, Philosophy & Art* (Temple Lodge, 2018).

'death'. The end of the earth started in the fifth post-Atlantean age and will be completed in the sixth and seventh ages. This is why we are now already living in the apocalyptic time and it is becoming apocalyptic or revelatory, more and more.

Another aspect of this, that brings us to the present time in a radical way, is what Rudolf Steiner refers to often, that since the end of the nineteenth century, which means from the beginning of the age of Michael and the New Age of Light, humanity has been unconsciously crossing the threshold of the spiritual world. He says in 1924, in another testamentary word, that humanity already lives on the other side of the threshold, and this is why we must have spiritual science, to bring this crossing and its meaning into full consciousness. And what is death if not crossing the threshold? It is a collective death process of humanity and planet Earth. As we saw above, after we die and enter Kamaloka, we see our lower self as it really is. This means that 33 years after humanity began to cross the threshold—to die—this being will appear, which we meet every time we die; a being that will appear in its final form at the end of the evolution of the earth. But this is the most important thing: it must not remain unconscious. We must consciously cope with it, confront it in full consciousness and recognize this being for what it really is, without illusions. The rise of this being from its imprisonment in the body after death must take place, in the present age of the consciousness soul, in full consciousness. And this should have happened in 1933, but did not.

This is why modern spiritual science was given to humanity by Michael from the beginning of the twentieth century, because when humanity begins to cross the threshold unconsciously, enough people must be fully conscious of this; enough people must *know* that we are crossing the threshold, that we are dying and must face the Lesser Guardian, and not continue to believe that we are still living physically as usual! If you die and don't notice it, which is the fate of millions of souls today, you don't know that you are dead, and you strive to continue to live your physical life as you did before. This causes great suffering for you and for the people you are connected with. And the same is true for humanity as a whole: because the crossing of the threshold remained unconscious for 10-20 years, you got the madness of WWI, and because it continued after 1933, the volcano broke loose, the abyss was opened, the first Beast was released and was unrecognized, and you got WWII, which is beyond the definitions of ordinary madness. The Beast was revealed, and because humanity rejected the spiritual knowledge of modern spiritual science, we had no clue what it represents, and we couldn't consciously face and cope with it at all! Rather, the Beast consciously faced and dealt with us. In our blind ignorance and pride, we believed that it represented our higher self, and have gladly identified with it and did what it demanded, that is, we totally followed our lowest instincts and desires.

Now we can understand what Rudolf Steiner meant when he said that before we can *rightly* perceive the etheric Christ, we must first *consciously cope* with the Beast. This means that we not only have to see and experience it, because its appearance will be a given fact, but we must have the spiritual knowledge to *recognize* who it is *in the real time of its appearance*. We must be able to recognize and name it, and if we do so, we would naturally exclaim: *Oy Vey'z Mir! Oy Gevalt!*[34] *This must be the Beast about which Rudolf Steiner spoke to us nine years ago!* And then the Beast will have lost its power over you, because you will no longer believe that it is your saviour; you will have realized that you must be its saviour, that is, the saviour of your lower self. Now you can recognize the Christ in the right way, because you know who the Beast is, and you

---

[34] In Yiddish it sounds better because it is a synthesis of the Hebrew and German languages.

know who the Christ is. When you can cope with the Beast in this way, recognizing it consciously, you can meet the etheric Christ in the right way, in full consciousness as well, and the whole history of the last century can take a totally different, positive turn.

Indeed, in any time other than ours, where we live under the absolute dominance of lies, this would have sounded obvious. A person must be able to recognize the truth, because it makes all the difference in the world if I think that what I am meeting is a human being, but is actually a bear; or if I believe it is a mouse, when it is actually an elephant! I will certainly behave differently on both occasions! In the moment that you realize: this is Ahriman, this is Lucifer, this is the first Beast, this is the second Beast, this is my neighbour—in this moment you also know what is to be done, and you act accordingly. And the moment you know it, you know how to handle it, and it cannot harm you; it cannot possess and manipulate you. You are free to develop your cognitive and moral forces and address the situation in the right way. Spiritual knowledge gives you freedom as the gift of the spirit of truth, and freedom lets you develop true love. And then you can also meet the higher spiritual forces in full consciousness and freedom. And this is what modern spiritual science should become one day: a living praxis, not mere theory.

So, all this could and should have happened before 1933. This was the main mission of spiritual science at the beginning of last century, to prepare humanity for this decisive event. But because spiritual science was rejected by humanity and Rudolf Steiner died in 1925, its development stopped and never made it to 1933. The tragic fate of humanity was sealed: we arrived at the most decisive moment of our present evolution in 1933 in spiritual blindness. And this must be understood as well: when you are blind, it is not only that you don't see the truth, you also cannot distinguish truth from falsehood, and not only that: you will unavoidably mistake and exchange truth for lies, and good for evil. In short, you will actualize the most profound reversal in our time and take the good for evil and evil for the highly cherished, worshipped good. And this reversal is the cardinal truth of modern history, as I showed in *The Event in History*,[35] and in the lecture from 2009 about 'The Beast and the Reversal'.[36] This is the fundamental spiritual, psychological, and social law of modern times: that all higher truths and spiritual forces are reversed into their opposites if human consciousness doesn't rise up to grasp them at their supersensible source. Therefore, in 1933 people named the Beast the Christ and named the Christ the Beast. This was the major reversal of all truths, which continues today as we speak, fulfilling in the most terrible way the essential truth of the reversal process in modern history. Karl Heyer wrote:

> The following word applies to the three ideals [of the French revolution]: *corruptio optimi fit pessima*—the reversal of the best leads to the worst. The higher a good that wants to be realized, the deeper the fall when it changes into the opposite. The more Michaelic the image, the more the dragon powers pervert the three ideals in order to fight the image through the counter-image.[37]

In *The Event in History*, I showed how the three heads of the first Beast rose up, reversing the threefold ideal of brotherhood, equality and liberty, and how all people worshipped its power in the west, east and in middle Europe. In the west, the Beast takes on the form of the American materialistic ideals: the capitalism that people worship as the power of redemption, the transformation of human nature through technology, overcoming all illnesses and death, and creating eternal life and paradise on the earth. In the east, the Beast

---

[35] *The Event in Science, History, Philosophy and Art* (Temple Lodge, 2018).
[36] *Spiritual Science in the 21st Century* (Temple Lodge, 2017).
[37] Karl Heyer, *Die Französische Revolution und Napoleon* (Verlag Freies Geistesleben, 1989).

was worshipped in the form of Bolshevism and communism, promising brotherhood and equality, and in middle Europe and Germany the Beast perverted the form of the chosen people from the Old Testament, rooted in blood and soil, in fascism and national socialism. And you can see how people were totally amazed when they saw the threefold Beast—in the west, the east, and the middle—worshipping and serving its goals with all their forces, and believing that this was the true Christ impulse, the Messiah, the benevolent *Führer*, the best economic, political and cultural life, that would lead us to the new Heaven and Earth.

This must be by now very familiar to us, dear friends, but we must contemplate the mysteries of historical and personal reversal repeatedly, from new points of view, because it is not only about the past century. The law of reversal is the apocalyptic secret of the present and future time, and it is here to stay with us until the end of the evolution of the earth.

Now, if you were thinking that what happened in 1933 and its aftermath was bad enough, you will be surprised again, dear friends. We spoke only about the *first* Beast and have yet to speak about the second. And here we must enter really deeply into dark regions, so let us strengthen our etheric hearts with the Christ-given forces of love, faith and hope, and fire them with Michaelic enthusiasm, to face the second Beast—and the union of the two—with active and creative courage.

In Nuremberg, Rudolf Steiner described the second Beast in the following way. As we saw, when the evolution of the earth is completed, the first Beast appears in the astral world, representing that part of humanity that rejected the Christ impulse. Above the fallen part of humanity appears the Imagination of the spiritualized humanity, in the picture of heavenly Jerusalem, which contains all the souls that transformed themselves through the Christ impulse. But the appearance of the first Beast will attract another cosmic being, who doesn't belong to the evolution of the earth. He comes from totally different worlds and streams of evolution that have nothing to do with the true evolution of the earth. And this being will be very satisfied, says Rudolf Steiner, to assimilate everything on the earth that rejected the Christ impulse. This being is the second Beast, the Sun demon, the Doppelgänger of Christ, called Sorat. Rudolf Steiner said it would feel very satisfied to nourish itself with the remains of the unredeemed humanity on the earth.

The connection of the second Beast to the first Beast is described in the thirteenth chapter of Revelation in these Imaginative pictures:

> Then I saw a second beast, coming out of the earth. It had two horns like a lamb, but it spoke like a dragon. It exercised all the authority of the first beast on its behalf, and made the earth and its inhabitants worship the first beast, whose fatal wound had been healed. And it performed great signs, even causing fire to come down from heaven to the earth in full view of the people. Because of the signs it was given power to perform on behalf of the first beast, it deceived the inhabitants of the earth. It ordered them to set up an image in honour of the beast who was wounded by the sword and yet lived. The second beast was given power to give breath to the image of the first beast, so that the image could speak and cause all who refused to worship the image to be killed. It also forced all people, great and small, rich and poor, free and slave, to receive a mark on their right hands or on their foreheads, so that they could not buy or sell unless they had the mark, which is the name of the beast or the number of its name. This calls for wisdom. Let the person who has insight calculate the number of the beast, for it is a human number. That number is 666.[38]

The second Beast makes all people worship the first Beast, whose mortal wound was magically healed, and uses its

---

[38] The Book of Revelation, 13:11-18.

magical power to enslave humanity to these forces. But what does it mean that it makes a living image of the first Beast and forces all humans to worship it? What is indicated here is the creation of the subhuman evil race, formed in the image of the unredeemed, fallen human nature. And the second Beast takes over all aspects of spiritual, cultural and social life. If you want to buy or sell, you have to inscribe in your body the sign or name of the beast to be part of its civilization. But what exactly is meant with the mysterious number, 666?

All cycles of time, from the smallest cycle of the seven years in our life to centuries and millennia and the evolution of the earth through the seven planetary stages from Saturn to Vulcan, are regulated by a sevenfold life process, the basic rhythm of all evolution in time. The number six is the last opportunity before the completion of each seven-year cycle, and therefore it is the last and decisive chance to complete the right development of each cycle. It is the last moment for transformation and redemption before this period is completed. If you count from Old Saturn to Vulcan, we are in the fourth planetary stage on the earth. Then comes Jupiter, the fifth and then Venus, the sixth stage of our evolution. The seventh and last planetary stage is Vulcan, whose full number is 777, the completion of the whole cosmic cycle and the beginning of a new one. Therefore, we should note that the last decisive number six appears in the sixth planetary incarnation of the earth, in Venus. When Venus evolution reaches its sixth age, and the sixth substage of this age, the number 666 will be fulfilled. Before then, all evil must have been transformed into higher good.

This means that our task is to redeem all evil before 666 is fulfilled. There should not remain any human being unredeemed after the end of Venus. But also, in smaller cycles whenever five and six appear, we are nearing the end and it becomes increasingly decisive. Because we live now in the fifth cultural epoch of the fifth post-Atlantean age, it is a strong double five. As we move to the next sixth cultural epoch, our post-Atlantean number will be 556, and the planetary number 456, and it will get hotter as we move on. You can feel, can't you, that it is getting hot under your seats when you contemplate this. In every year, decade and century it's getting hotter!

This is the esoteric formula that governs inwardly and qualitatively, the essence of all evolution in time, and it should not be taken to mean a mere abstract 'law'. If you meditate on it intensely, you will experience how it works in your individual biography and human history. Now that we are better acquainted with what those priests knew, who listened to Rudolf Steiner in September 1924, we can also better experience their second major surprise, when Rudolf Steiner told them that the second Beast would also appear at the end of the twentieth century, in 1998:

> We are now facing the age of the third 666—1998. At the end of this century we will come to the time when Sorat will again raise its head most strongly from the tides of evolution, where it will be the adversary of that sight of the Christ, which those people who are prepared for it will already have in the first half of the twentieth century when the etheric Christ becomes visible. It will take only 2/3 of this century until Sorat will raise its head in a mighty way... There are already today developments that rage against the spiritual. But these are only the first seeds.[39]

Just imagine this: until this moment, we could continue our sleep rather comfortably, knowing that the first Beast will only appear far in the future, at the end of the evolution of the earth and the second Beast after it. And now—lo and behold!—we are told that the first Beast will appear in 1933, in only nine years, and that it must be recognized before the etheric Christ can be rightly grasped; and we would then remember that a week earlier, Rudolf Steiner already told

---

[39] Lecture of 12 September 1924 (GA 346).

us that the second Beast will raise its head in 1998, fighting against the new revelation of the etheric Christ. Suddenly, if you were listening to these lectures, you would have found yourself confronted by the most unsettling prediction, that in 1933 to 1998 the two Beasts will intervene together in the immediate present evolution of humanity, not only at its end. And please mark the tight timetable of these events: the last lecture on Revelation to the priests was given on 22 September, and on 28 September, on Michaelmas eve, 1924, Rudolf Steiner delivered his last address and on 30 March, 1925, he took leave of the physical world!

This is the reason we felt obliged to at least indicate in some words in *The Twilight and Resurrection of Humanity* how the two Beasts have been working together since 1998, and how at the end of the twentieth century, the prediction of Chapter 13 was fulfilled, and the two Beasts took over our entire civilization, because the culmination of the Michaelic movement didn't take place at the end of the century. Rather, the 'culmination' of Ahriman's century did occur and he could offer his power ceremonially to the two Beasts, who took it over from him. Since then we truly are living in 'the grave of civilization', predicted by Rudolf Steiner if the Michaelic plan for the twentieth century failed.

You can well imagine that I have been particularly interested in these questions, because once you experience how the two Beasts united their forces at the end of the century, you are faced with great difficulties. You must find the inner cognitive and moral strength to face this reality, to recognize it and cope with it, if you want to find the right way to experience the death and resurrection of the etheric Christ inside the grave of civilization, and help Him lift the heaviest stone: the dominance of the two Beasts, who naturally fight vehemently against any effort to do so.

This is where we stand now. This is truly what is happening. And true spiritual science has the task to investigate reality and communicate this knowledge to the people who want to receive it. The good news that we described from various points in *The Twilight and Resurrection of Humanity*, is that in the twenty-first century, after Chapter 13 of Revelation is completed in our time and the two Beasts are beginning to dominate human evolution, we also receive the first glimpse of what is described in Chapter 14. This contains the first Imagination of the spiritual movement of our time, of those who remained loyal to Michael through the apocalypse of the twentieth century, even if to begin with, it is a rather invisible underground etheric movement. It is called *Zion* in this chapter, and the inspired Wachowski brothers also applied it to name the surviving human enclave in the centre of the earth in *The Matrix* trilogy. This is the reversed ahrimanic Imagination of the New Jerusalem, the seed of future Jupiter, which lives however not in the middle of the old earth, but in the middle of the new etheric earthly-human Sun.

It is important to understand the true meaning of what John says in Chapter 14, but this will only be possible if we understand the history of the twentieth century in the light of Chapters 12 and 13. In Chapter 14 he says, 'Then I looked, and there before me was the Lamb, standing on Mount Zion, and with him 144,000 who had his name and his Father's name written on their foreheads.' This means that these people could marshal the forces of the Christ, actualize them to develop the forces of spiritual cognition, which means, to imprint Christ's name, the power of His I AM, on their foreheads. In other words, the forces of love and compassion, of true healing, could become so active and creative in their hearts, that they could recognize the Christ and not mistake Him and reverse Him into the opposite to worship the Beasts instead. They could consciously overcome the power of the Beasts and allow the living stream of Christ-Michael to incarnate and develop on earth, inside the grave of civilization. The Apocalypse of St John emphasizes it again in this passage, by saying that 'They follow the Lamb wherever he goes'. And this is precisely the goal of the School of Spiritual Science in the twenty-first century, to 'follow the Lamb wherever he goes'. And John also describes the global nature of this School, which is essential for our work in this century, namely, that Michael's true pupils are 'purchased from among mankind and offered as the first fruits to God and the Lamb'. From all the nations of the world the future brotherhood of Philadelphia, of the sixth cultural epoch, will be assembled, the potent human seed of which must be prepared in the present age of Michael.

The goal of the movement of Michael in the twenty-first century, the second, middle century of his present age, will only be understood, if we realize that its living centre is the new appearance of the etheric Christ, discovered and experienced through the new Michaelic impulse. And this points clearly to our immediate task in the coming 2020s and 30s: to build this community on 'Mount Zion', around 'the Lamb', on such strong foundations that it will continue to grow and become stronger, widening the bridge to the etheric world each day, and letting the temple of the earthly-human Sun become visible among humans, despite all hindrances, in the first half of the century.

Now that we have placed before us the essential characteristics of the two Beasts and their role in the apocalypse of the age of Michael, I would like to turn your attention to one specific detail, that has central significance to the question of ahrimanic and Michaelic immortality. My research was directed to this mystery once I began to investigate the union of the two Beasts after 1998 and its connection to the project of ahrimanic immortality. The problem I faced at the end of last century and the turn to the new century and millennium, was how to find the way to the new revelation of the Christ in the twenty-first century, which was suppressed by this union. The goal of this research was to find the exact spot, the exact entry point, through which one could break through this double deadlock, to find the narrow path that leads to the new Christ impulse in the twenty-first century. Again and again, this research led me to the question of how to build the individual and communal etheric body, the bridge and chalice that must be created in this century. I realized that I must focus my attention on the Imagination of the mortally wounded and magically healed head of the first Beast, which the second Beast, Sorat, manipulates with such horrific skill. I discovered that in the mystery of this wound, the key is to be found that is required to grasp how the two Beasts united their forces at the end of last century and founded their global domination of humanity in the twenty-first century.

I remember vividly how, as the twentieth century drew to its close, I realized more and more that the knowledge of this key is the precondition for developing the forces required to overcome this union and answer the ahrimanic immortality with the Christ-given immortality of Michael. I discovered that the new impulse of the Christ in the twenty-first century is active most intensively in the healing of this wound and if we want to find it by the middle of the century, we can only find it there. Therefore, I was pursuing these investigations with great intensity in the first decade of this century.

On the one hand, I had to deepen my research into the occult history of humanity in the twentieth century, in the light of the activity and union of the two Beasts and the formation of our collective wound, and on the other hand, to delve deeper into my own lower nature, to acquaint myself more intimately with the same process in my bodies, to investigate in detail the formation of the 'wound of Amfortas' in myself. Some of the results of this research, concerning the Parsifal-Amfortas duality and its healing in my biographical development, I described in the first lecture of *The Twilight and Resurrection of Humanity*. In this manner, I could learn first-hand to know the three basic elements of the mystery of the wound: first, the origins, formation and essential nature of the wound; second, the secrets of its unlawful healing, in which the two Beasts unite their forces and attain their greatest power; and third, the portal that leads to its rightful healing, through the forces of the etheric Christ. In the third volume of *The Modern Christ Experience and the Knowledge Drama of the Second Coming*, I describe this research in detail. In our lecture tomorrow, I will briefly indicate some of its features.

At the close of this lecture, I want to address a concern that may naturally arise in your hearts, when you listen to our lectures about ahrimanic immortality and the mission of the two Beasts in the present apocalyptic age of Michael. You may say: You have communicated spiritual knowledge about so many bad things in these lectures! How are we to deal with this knowledge in a way that will enhance our faith in the good, and fire our enthusiasm to actualize it in our community building? To this I would reply that the attainment of spiritual knowledge in spiritual scientific research, is in itself a positive, creative undertaking, which is well grounded in the positive forces of the good, and is absolutely necessary, if human evolution is to find the right path in the twenty-first century.

The reason is that spiritual research engages all our human forces, sets in motion all the forces of our souls, quickens and awakens all the forces of our spirit. And this has significance not only for us as humans, but also for the spiritual beings of the higher hierarchies, who remained loyal to Michael and humanity, despite our continuous man-made twilight and fall into the abyss and grave of civilization. What is discovered by the free spiritual activity of the human soul, requires the previous spiritualization of our ordinary thinking, feelings and will forces. And what we spiritualize from our soul life on the earth, the gods are most ardently seeking, to be able to help us in our present apocalyptic travails. They can only help humanity if humanity becomes truly co-creative with them, if humans activate the deepest forces of their beings and raise them up to the gods, from the grave and abyss into which we are rapidly sinking. What humans discover when they investigate the mysteries of humanity, the earth and cosmos, has vital meaning and great significance not only for us here on the earth, but also for our spiritual colleagues and mentors in the spiritual world.

But you can nevertheless contend that the gods must know these mysteries very well already. Why should they care if we also know them? What spiritual science discovers, you may say, is not new for them. Why do they need us to produce spiritual knowledge, spiritual art, and spiritual deeds of love on earth, if they possess so much spiritual knowledge and love?

Well, these objections are justified, especially if we recall that as early as 1924, Rudolf Steiner says that even some of the closest gods have given up their faith in humanity—and this was before the horrors we accomplished between 1933-1945 and up to 1998. But dear friends, for Michael, who remained loyal to humanity and the earth, because he is eternally loyal to the Christ, who made the earth His new cosmic abode, the fruits of our free spiritual activity make all the difference in the world! For Michael's main concern is the question: Will humanity exist tomorrow and after tomorrow in a way that corresponds to the will of Christ? Will the earth be redeemed, or will it sink down with humanity into the abyss and be totally taken over by the two Beasts? *This is the question that the Michaelic gods ask us.* This they cannot answer. Humans have to answer this.

When we answer this question with all our creative Michaelic enthusiasm, they can join the work and help us, and we can work together with them. Otherwise, they cannot reach humanity. They see humanity falling below them into the abyss and their hearts and hands cannot reach us. But for the twilight of humanity in the twentieth century to be followed by the resurrection of humanity in the twenty-first century, free and creative, cognitive and moral human activity is required. And this is the task of the movement of Michael in this century.

After we have visited the Church of St Georg in Reichenau, we may find the required forces to address in this spirit some aspects of what Rudolf Steiner said in this region a century ago, and bring it *up to date*. That is, we can lift it up to the spiritual world and reconnect spiritual science with the present activity and goals of the Time Spirit, Michael, so that he can breathe and weave in our midst.

Lecture 4

Follow This Good Star

Überlingen, 4 November 2022

In our recent lectures we had to deal with central questions of human evolution which are continuously developing, and we have not had enough time to address more specific questions of knowledge and life. I hope that the time will come in which we will be able to speak about specific questions of life, for example, about the connection to the dead.

The connection to the dead is of fundamental importance to our work in so many ways. One could say that it is closely related to the central spiritual trunk and is not another branch on the tree. When we are active in the school of Michael in which we live and weave, if we truly feel the presence of the school of Michael in and around us, then we shall also feel the company of the so-called dead souls. This is actually a terribly false expression, for the livingly awakened souls who live in the spiritual world are among the most active and creative participants in the supersensible school of Michael. And we could feel the living presence of these awakened souls when we visited the Church of St Georg in Reichenau in Lake Constance.

After observing the wonderful ethereal paintings on the walls of the church, which depict Christ's deeds of healing and resurrection described in the Gospels, we found out that a Franciscan Capuchin monk named Gideon Spicker, who died in 1912, is buried there and that he lived most of his life in Reichenau. He is an exceedingly interesting personality. As a religious person and philosopher, he became deeply interested in questions of science and the connection between religion, philosophy and science. In 1872 he wrote a book about the British philosopher, Shaftesbury, in which we find the following statement:

> If science is the knowledge of things and if philosophy is ultimately this knowledge, then the actual study of man is man himself and philosophy's highest goal is self-knowledge or Anthroposophy.[40]

Now you would recall that Rudolf Steiner said that he took the name of anthroposophy from the title of a book written by his teacher in Vienna, Robert Zimmermann, in 1882. But if you compare Zimmermann's philosophy to Spicker, you would say that Spicker was much closer to anthroposophy. And Rudolf Steiner was so impressed by his thinking and personality, that when he wrote the Mystery Dramas, he found in Spicker the archetype for the character of the scientist, Doctor Strader. We cannot go into this subject in greater detail right now, but if you recall who Doctor Strader was and the role he plays in the Mystery Dramas, you will also remember that in the fourth drama he suddenly dies. Before he died, he experienced a decisive crisis in his personal and spiritual life. Strader's life and tasks are deeply connected to the mission of spiritual science and are therefore of great interest to our work.

We know that all his life Strader was struggling with the connection of natural science and spiritual science. This was the leitmotif for his life. As a scientist he had to struggle with Ahriman, just like his counterpart, Professor Capesius, the humanist, was struggling with Lucifer. As you know, Ahriman's greatest 'daymare', which he dreads most intensely, is the wedding of science and spirit: the creation of spiritual science. Strader's struggle with Ahriman helped Benedictus to achieve his ultimate victory over Ahriman. The second thing

---

[40] Gideon Spicker, *Die Philosophie des Grafen von Shaftesbury nebst Einleitung und Kritik über das Verhältniss der Religion zur Philosophie und der Philosophie zur Wissenschaft*, Freiburg i. B. 1872, p. 319.

that is characteristic for Strader is his relationship with the only person in the Mystery Dramas, Theodora, who experiences a prevision of the coming appearance of the etheric Christ. Later on, the two meet and fall in love and then Theodora suddenly dies, and this is a great shock for Strader, and you could say that he dies following her. So, we have before us a human being who is struggling with Ahriman and the transformation of natural science into spiritual science, who exclaims, when he experiences Theodora's testimony, in the face of the reservations of others: 'Yet we have a fact before us!' His destiny brought him to feel Theodora's vision very deeply. But it remains to begin with an external fact. It is only through Theodora that he can begin to experience the spirit more directly, and then she dies and his connection to the spiritual world for the time being is cut off.

Now, in his previous incarnation in the Middle Ages, Strader was the Jew, Simon, who rejected the Christ when Christ approached him. In the Mystery Dramas, he comes very close to the first vision of the etheric Second Coming through Theodora, and he doesn't reject it out of hand, but then she dies. He feels that he has lost this opportunity, in the moment when he would have perhaps begun to approach Christ more closely. And if you study the biography of Gideon Spicker, you will see that his life's struggle was about the connection between religion and science. As we could gather from his words cited above, he was actually searching to attain the new spiritual knowledge of man and the universe that can bridge religion and science, and he called it anthroposophy. The deeper you get to know his life, the more you can understand why he became the archetype of Strader in the Mystery Dramas. His is indeed such a remarkable destiny in many, many respects!

It is also remarkable to note what Rudolf Steiner has to say about it years later. He says, 'You know that Strader had to die, because Gideon Spicker died in 1912.'[41] And the reason why this was so, is even more remarkable. This is important when we raise the question of the connection with the so-called dead and strive to get closer to the riddle of destiny about why Spicker lived in Reichenau. Rudolf Steiner says that some souls, after they cross the threshold, become much more alive and interesting after death than they were in their physical life. He said: I cannot continue to write about Strader in the physical world, while I see how alive his archetype is becoming in the spiritual world. Strader in the physical world was a mere shadow in comparison to his living spiritual archetype! Therefore, he had to die as well. It is highly interesting what Rudolf Steiner says 'about the other characters I planned to continue to write', because he was planning the next Mystery Dramas in which the life of the main characters would unfold further, and this would not be a problem, because their spiritual archetypes were not standing before him in such a living way as the soul of Gideon Spicker.

Now we can ask, how is all of this connected to our present tasks?

Consider the Spicker-Strader archetype, whose karma and mission is played out in the field of tension between science, spiritual science and the new revelation of the etheric Christ, in which 'dark Ahriman, spreading chaos' is constantly hindering human evolution in the present age of Michael. If you do so, you will certainly feel why it pertains so directly to our work, and what another source of inspiration we have, if we draw closer to him, among the powerfully active souls in the spiritual world.

To understand this fully, let us connect all that we have said in the lectures contained in the present book. Let us

---

[41] GA 239, lecture 1.

remember what was covered in the lectures from 2017 about ahrimanic and Michaelic immortality. This can also serve as an extension to some of the subjects dealt with in my books, *The Twilight and Resurrection of Humanity*, *The Event in Science, History, Philosophy and Art*, and *The Spiritual Event of the Twentieth Century*.

When you contemplate this subject from ever new perspectives, you feel the need to go from the St Georg church in Reichenau to the small town of St Gallen, and to what took place there in a most decisive month and year of the last century. In April 1917, America declared war on Germany and entered the First World War, and on 3 November, the final stage of the Bolshevik Revolution occurred in Russia. This sealed the tragic fate of Europe in the twentieth century, one of the last chapters of which is presently being written in the war in Ukraine, while the Balfour Declaration issued in London on 2 November 1917, set the stage for developments in Palestine and the Middle East that continue today. Long and far-reaching occult hands are working here, which plan and regulate the ahrimanic course of history in terms of centuries and cultural epochs, not mere decades. Therefore, every word that Rudolf Steiner said in 1917 from beginning to the end, and all his efforts to avert this tragedy, must be studied very carefully, and also understood in the light of what he communicated in his lecture in St Gallen.

I will give a very short summary of some of the main issues of the lecture from 16 November, 1917, but be reminded that it contains many other subjects that we cannot explicate in greater detail now.[42]

The central communication made in this lecture is that incarnating human souls are not fully embodied and cannot inhabit some lower parts of the body. There remains a gap not filled by the soul due to the fact that our physical body

---

[42] GA 178.

is becoming increasingly hardened, and the soul cannot master it. And this gives the opportunity for the ahrimanic Doppelgänger to enter our body and take possession of the subconscious body and soul regions that we cannot fill with our soul. And Rudolf Steiner says that this being is the cause of all the organic illnesses and sicknesses of the human being. (It should be noted that the part of the human soul that cannot be fully incarnated remains outside and becomes possessed by a luciferic Doppelgänger, about which we cannot speak now.) Rudolf Steiner adds that the ahrimanic Doppelgänger was known in the past in some European mysteries, and they discovered that the best way to investigate the source of inner illnesses and their healing was to travel to North America, where the forces of magnetism and electricity, to which the Doppelgänger is connected, are most active. By means of Norwegian and Viking ships, they travelled to America, studied the Doppelgänger and the illnesses and brought the knowledge of healing back to Europe. All the basic principles of ancient mystery medicine came from this source.

The Irish monks who established the influential esoteric centre in Reichenau in the first centuries of Christianity, which gave rise to such a wonderful religious, artistic and scientific life, which flourished in the ninth through eleventh centuries, brought with them also this knowledge of healing. The atmosphere of healing that one can still experience in the entire region of Lake Constance, is an echo from this impulse, because in these centuries this knowledge was still alive.

However, what Rudolf Steiner then adds in this lecture, is of great significance for our present time. He says that the Irish monks also knew that Christianity and European civilization could not bring about the required development of the ego, as long as the ancient spiritual connection to America existed and the knowledge of the Doppelgänger was still alive. And they brought it about, through the impulse of Roman Christianity, that America and the secrets of the Doppelgänger were intentionally suppressed and forgotten, to be rediscovered only after the free human individuality began to develop in the fifteenth century in the age of the consciousness soul. Then Europe and America could be connected again. Yes, this also belongs to this mystery, dear friends, that in 1917 the US entered the war in Europe, and would not leave Europe ever again! Rudolf Steiner said that such individualities as Columbanus and his pupil, Gallus, who founded the city of St Gallen, where he was speaking about the mysteries of the ahrimanic Doppelgänger, are also connected to the karma that came about because they suppressed this impulse. They knew that for Europe to fulfil its mission, America had to be forgotten for a long enough time, but with it the esoteric knowledge about the Doppelgänger, illness and healing was also lost.

Consider the significance of the time in which the lecture in St Gallen was delivered, and you will see how karma works through the ages, weaving together threads that are spread far apart in time and space.

When I spoke in Stuttgart about ahrimanic and Michaelic immortality a century later, in November 2017, I described the developments and consequences of what Rudolf Steiner said a century ago. Think about it: in April 1917, the western aspect of the Beast rose from the west and entered Europe through the American powers; in November its eastern head appeared in the form of Bolshevism, which stormed towards central Europe from the east, and in the heart of Europe, in Germany, the third aspect of the Beast arose. In this moment Rudolf Steiner goes to St Gallen and reveals the mysteries of the forgotten Doppelgänger, illness and healing. And therefore, he said, 'You could say that I have spoken here today in this way, because the *genius loci*, the spirit being of this place required it of me.' This offers you a concrete example of how real karma works, not in mere abstract concepts, but in all reality, because what must be shut down in one age, must be opened again in the next one, and the spirit of the place in which the connection with America was severed, and the Doppelgänger forgotten, asked Rudolf Steiner in November 1917 to once again open up the secrets that were closed in this place in the past. And this is also the place where the archetype of Strader was struggling with Ahriman and with the future appearance of the etheric Christ, through the life of Gideon Spicker.

As we showed in the lecture yesterday, this is the great apocalyptic question with which the last century ended and the twenty-first century and the third millennium began, which is also the existential question of the age of Michael as a whole: Will humanity be able to perceive the Second Coming of the etheric Christ and consciously confront and cope with not only the first Beast that rose in 1933, but with the detrimental fact that since 1998 both Beasts are working together? The question is more difficult and crucial for the twenty-first century than the testamentary words Rudolf Steiner presented in September 1924 to the priests. The main difference is that he spoke *before* the rise of the *first* Beast in 1933, and we live *after* the rise of the *two* Beasts in 1933 and 1998 and must confront in full consciousness their union and conquest of human civilization since 1998. We must therefore rephrase what Rudolf Steiner said in September 1924, that 'before humanity can meet the Christ, it must consciously confront the Beast that will arise from the abyss in 1933'. What is similar between the beginning of the twentieth and the twenty-first centuries is that Rudolf Steiner pointed to the imminent appearance of the etheric Christ before the middle of the twentieth century, and we look forward to an intensified renewal of the Christ event before the middle of the twenty-first century.

Therefore, today in 2022 we must say that 'before humanity can perceive the new revelation of the etheric Christ in the twenty-first century, it must first cope with and confront *the united power of the two Beasts,* which already fully control all aspects of modern life in the grave of civilization'. Since the end of the last century the two Beasts have been working together, supported by Lucifer and Ahriman from the flanks and the Asuras in the middle, and they rule humanity as it sinks ever deeper into the abyss. Over against this free fall, the mightiest protesting action of Michael stands out, heralding the new Christ event of the twenty-first century. Dear friends, we must say it today, in November 2022, in all seriousness, because this event of the twenty-first century is situated in the middle of the present age of Michael, in its crucial apocalyptic moment, and it confronts us as a significant and shattering world-and-human question.

To understand the full significance of this question and find the narrow path that alone can lead us to its resolution, let us review again the mystery of the miraculous healing of the wound of sexuality and mortality as the ultimate source of ahrimanic immortality and its Michaelic redemption. This leads us back to the inspiring spiritual being of the lake of Constance district, which has placed new requirements before us. To address his new request, we have to again visit Rudolf Steiner's lecture in St Gallen and be reminded of what we said in the earlier lectures of this book about the ahrimanic Doppelgänger.

The first and most general goal of Ahriman is to make life between birth and death in the physical world so materialistic that after death, people will not realize that they live in the spiritual world at all and will continue to adhere as strongly as before to physical life. We spoke about the role of the technological singularity in realizing this ahrimanic goal, which we called 'Ahriman's kindergarten', since it is a preparation for his elementary and high school in the twenty-second and twenty-third centuries and his coming incarnation. We pointed out that according to Ray Kurzweil, by 2045 full bodily, soul and cognitive immersion in infinitely intelligent virtual reality will be possible. Now, if you are totally surrendering to this materialistic life, with all the forces of your thinking, feeling and will, it affects your etheric body also in sleep. Because your etheric body is filled with ahrimanic forces, bereft of any spiritual concepts, feelings and will impulses, ahrimanic beings use the time in which your astral body and ego are outside the physical and etheric bodies, to replace your God-given etheric body with their sub-earthly etheric body. In this way, already during earthly life, the etheric body is so hardened that when you die, it does not dissolve in the cosmic ether and remains bound to the earth, chaining you to the earth as the heaviest burden even after the three days after death have passed. And this means that after death, the soul remains bound to the earth through the hardened etheric body and does not wish to enter Kamaloka in the astral world and ascend to the spiritual world, to prepare and realize her next incarnation. In this case, the continuation of karma from one incarnation to the next would have been abolished and the true spiritual immortality would have been replaced by reversed, ahrimanic immortality, and the soul would be cut off forever from her true human destiny and vocation.

Now, if these conditions are fulfilled, the Doppelgänger can finally attain his long sought for desire to remain with the human soul when she goes through the portal of death, uniting with her in the etheric world, and possessing her also after death. And I pointed out that this constitutes a wholly new kind of caricatured essence exchange between the Doppelgänger and the human soul, a reciprocally actualized ahrimanic immortality that merges the human soul and the Doppelgänger in an unholy union. The human soul becomes ahrimanized, the ahrimanic Doppelgänger becomes ensouled, so that the ahrimanic immortality of the human soul and the ensouled immortality of the ahrimanic Doppelgänger become one and the same.

Let us be aware, however, that for the ahrimanic forces that strive to impose ahrimanic immortality on human souls, all this is only the means for attaining still another, far reaching universal goal: to suppress the etheric Second Coming of Christ that started in 1933, to take over the etheric sphere in which the etheric Christ was supposed to appear, and replace Him by one of the strongest ahrimanic companions. This being can be characterized as the anti-Christ, or which is the same, as the ahrimanic Doppelgänger of the etheric Christ. The significance of this to the project of ahrimanic immortality and the striving of the Doppelgänger will be immediately clear, if we consider that Rudolf Steiner said that the reason why up to November 1917 the Doppelgänger could not yet fulfil his desire was the power of Christ flowing from the Mystery of Golgotha. But since 1933 Ahriman has succeeded in suppressing Christ's appearance in human consciousness, replacing Him by his ahrimanic Doppelgänger and taking over His sphere of life in the etheric world for himself and his hosts. The forces of the first Mystery of Golgotha were no longer able to be received by humanity, because since 1933 they can only be received through the new revelation of the etheric Christ. As was also described in *The Spiritual Event of the Twentieth Century*, for the first time since the Mystery of Golgotha, humanity was cut away from the Christ impulse. And this is what finally allowed both the individual and global ahrimanic doubles to attain their sought for immortality and victory, because the power of Christ that prevented it until 1933 was removed.

In other words, according to carefully conducted spiritual scientific investigations, we must say that what Rudolf

Steiner said in St Gallen on 16 November, 1917, must be updated. This disclosure is what the *genius loci* of this region requires from us now. The time is now ripe to describe these things in greater detail. One must point out that after the etheric Christ was replaced by His ahrimanic Doppelgänger, His sphere of life forces, the planetary etheric ring, to which we have often referred, was suppressed and hidden from human consciousness and replaced by an ahrimanic planetary etheric sphere. It has been forming itself from the ahrimanized human etheric bodies, becoming available in great numbers since 1933, increasing rapidly through 1998, and multiplied exponentially and disseminated globally since then. Many millions of human souls are already going through a totally ahrimanized physical life and death process, on such a mass scale, and this deadened etheric substance is the power by means of which ahrimanic immortality is sealed. In this way, the wound of sexuality and mortality that appears in one of the heads of the first Beast, and represents the lower self of humanity, is miraculously healed, because mortality was transformed into ahrimanic immortality. This is the process through which the realized goal of ahrimanic immortality has safeguarded the attainment of the goal of the two Beasts.

What I described above: the mystery of the two Beasts, the wound, and its connection to the project of ahrimanic immortality, is indicated clearly in Revelation, if we know how to read it in accord with the signs of the time. After the victory of Ahriman over humanity in the twentieth century is described in Chapter 12, the rise and joint dominance of the two Beasts is described in Chapter 13, and we showed that it began in 1998. In Revelation 13, verse 4, we read about the transition from the rule of Ahriman to the world dominance of the two Beasts; that 'people worshipped the dragon because he had given authority to the Beast, and they also worshipped the Beast and asked, "Who is like the Beast? Who can wage war against it?"'. This was the link that I was searching for, that discloses the mystery of the connection between the accomplished ahrimanic immortality of the individual soul and of humanity, the suppression of the etheric Christ impulse as a crowning ahrimanic achievement in the twentieth century, and the formation of the tightly closed wound of mortality, which has allowed the two Beasts to dominate all areas of life since the beginning of the twenty-first century.

Let us recap what we said recently in Sweden, when we pointed out that an important key to the understanding of the way the two Beasts work together and how to confront and recognize their cooperation, is connected to the mystery of the wound of sexuality and mortality. In *The Modern Christ Experience and the Knowledge Drama of the Second Coming*, I describe in detail how the wound is uncovered and healed in the human constitution. There I address, beside the luciferic-ahrimanic challenge, specifically the meaning of the new intervention of the Asuras in human evolution, and how they serve the goals of Sorat. This mystery is deeply connected to the question of how this wound can be healed in the right way, as opposed to the false miraculous healing offered by the two Beasts, which has become the principle of our civilization in all fields of science, technology, social, cultural and religious life. When I spoke about the meaning of ahrimanic immortality in 2017, I didn't mention the Asuras and the two Beasts explicitly, but the power that directs, from behind the occult scenes, the project of ahrimanic immortality, is the power of the two Beasts, working through the Asuras, and this means that ahrimanic immortality, if we recognize its deeper causes, is based on the miraculously healed wound.

What is the wound in the sense of Revelation? It is what makes us mortal. Why are we mortal? We are mortal because at the end of Lemuria, the original human being, *Adam Kadmon*, who represented the wholeness of cosmic life, who was an immortal eternal being, was divided into two opposite beings, each of which possessed only half of the immortal forces. Out of Adam, Eve was created; the original spiritual unity was broken, and they became mortal. The original holistic being of Adam Kadmon never died, but propagated its etheric and later its very delicate physical body, as today lower organisms and plants do, not through sexual reproduction, but in a pure vegetative, that is, spiritual way. We were in this sense immortal beings, endowed with very dim Imaginative consciousness, when this decisive event took place that led to the division of the sexes, the separation of the human constitution into the masculine and the feminine bodies. This division caused a veritable wound in both sexes, which in man is more etheric but which is physically visible in the bleeding wound of the female body. From that moment each male or female body had only half of the life forces of the former holistic body, and this made us mortal because the half-living body doesn't have enough life forces to keep living and therefore it must die, after it has exhausted the forces it brought from the life before birth in the spiritual world.

We are mortally wounded beings, that is, we die because we possess in our male and female bodies only half of the original amount of life forces. And this divided body is the wound of sexuality and mortality that appears in our lower nature—represented by the first Beast—as the mortally wounded 'head' that was miraculously, magically, healed. If you contemplate this mystery in the light of the Second Coming of the etheric Christ, working through the being of the Nathanic Jesus and radiating through the youth and healing-bringing forces of the Northern spirit, Vidar, you will experience the solution of this mystery, because you will experience how the wound of sexuality and mortality can be healed in the right way. You will experience, in and through the appearance, words and deeds of the etheric Christ, as I also showed in *The Three Meetings*, the being that not only preserves the original, pre-sexual and virgin wholeness of the human body, but demonstrates how humans can actualize this healing actively, in the present, and restore and resurrect the pristine, holistic human nature in all its glory and virginity. If you experience this mystery, which is part of the mysteries of the Second Coming in the present age of Michael, you will come to the following realization.

You will realize that this is the key to the riddle of the wounded head of the first Beast and its manipulation by the second Beast, the Sun demon, Sorat. We are told that it was mortally wounded and miraculously healed, and the power emanating from this magical healing fascinated and enslaved humanity. As we read in Revelation yesterday, Sorat is using this fascination to seduce humanity further. He makes humanity worship the first Beast and then creates a new being as an image of the Beast, the template of the fallen human race, in which the transmuted human being will incarnate, who has become ahrimanically, beastly, immortal. When you investigate these riddles, you are always led to this central mystery of the wound of sexuality, mortality and ahrimanic immortality, because this is where the two Beasts are unfolding their strongest forces, to take over and transform human civilization into a place in which the new fallen human race is formed. And the proper healing of this wound is the creative deed that constitutes Michaelic immortality in the present age of Michael. If you meditate on this for a long time, if you really enter with all the forces of your soul and heart into this mystery, you find yourself in the centre of the main activity and work of the etheric Christ impulse and school of Michael since the end of the twentieth century and the beginning of the twenty-first century.

In other words, if you do so, Michael leads you to Vidar, the being who serves as the living etheric form in which the etheric Christ is incorporating Himself, protecting and supporting the Nathanic Jesus being. This is the immortal source of pure virgin life, which nourishes the power for humanity to grow younger and serves most closely in this capacity the healing impulses of the etheric Christ. Kindly be reminded of Rudolf Steiner's exclamation in Oslo in June 1910, 'The etheric form is alive!' to which we dedicated the entire lecture cycle published in *The Twilight and Resurrection of Humanity*. In this etheric form and body, through which the etheric Christ appears, we find the key to the mystery of the wound of sexuality and mortality, and the attainment of ahrimanic and Michaelic immortality. When we confront in full consciousness the significance and consequences of what happened on earth and in the etheric world ever since 1933-1945, and the unification of the two Beasts in 1998, we see that they work most intensively on the wicked so-called 'healing' of the wound and reap its benefits in the form of the fast-spreading disaster of ahrimanic immortality.

In my investigations of the mysteries of this totally unique etheric body, I could also discover that this anti-Christ ahrimanic planetary etheric ring, which constitutes an entire subhuman, subterranean, etheric world, was completed in 1998-2001, when the forces of the first Beast that rose from the abyss in 1933 united fully with the forces of the second Beast after 1998. You can call it the planetary ring of ahrimanic immortality that miraculously heals and tightly closes the mortal wound of the old, dying earth. In this regard, it is not without relevance to mention what I remarked in a footnote to *The Twilight and Resurrection of Humanity*, concerning the occult meaning of the planned destruction of the Twin Towers in New York City on 11 September, 2001. I said that it instigated a global celebration, broadcast live *for all to see, so that they could fear and obey the masters of this world*, to exhibit the global fearful victory and dominance through all venues of global media; a bloody demonstration of the capacities of the coming civilization of the Beasts. But this evil deed was counteracted by the loving sacrifice of 3000 souls, who died in its flames, took it into themselves, and spiritualized it in real time as well. But this profound side of the externally shocking event was naturally never broadcast! This is also the reason why we *had* to celebrate the spiritual founding of our school in ground zero and plant this potent seed of redemption in the deep wound opened in the heart of the earth through the tremendous tremor caused by the bombing.

In doing this, we followed the call of the 3000 courageous human souls and the vast cloud of all the sacrificially departed souls in the last century, supported by all the Michaelic beings, illumined and blessed by the resurrected etheric Christ in their midst. The immensely powerful physical shock of the consciously planned and executed airborne bombing and ground demolition of the Twin Towers and the World Trade Center, caused a real tremor, a real earthquake, which practically cracked open the earth in this place and moment. The Christ forces of resurrection and healing, working from the centre of the earth, used it to emerge more vigorously than they could do before, to become available in the twenty-first century as never before, for the building of the earthly-human Sun.

Only in the 12 years, 1933-1945, could one perceive such stark contrasts standing one over against the other: the demonic performance and jubilation of all the adversarial forces, gathered around Sorat and his black subterranean sun, and the new, gently life and light-giving earthly-human Sun, heralded by the risen etheric Christ, revealing a new age of Christed human evolution.

Especially in the forces of the earth in eastern North America could we experience first-hand the involvement of the Doppelgänger in the project of ahrimanic immortality and the victory of the Beasts. It is comforting to know—at least for the best half of our school members—that Rudolf Steiner said that 'this ideal of ahrimanic immortality can be appropriately followed only by the male population'. This is also part of the mystery of the division of the sexes and the right and wrong healing of the wound of mortality referred to above, which we cannot explicate further now. You know that the male constitution has fallen below the human level, into the domain of Ahriman, and the female constitution remained above it, and comes under the domain of Lucifer. This will help you understand why the female body, which is softer and more spiritual, cannot help Ahriman in achieving this ahrimanic immortality. Ahriman influences the male body, and Lucifer the body of the woman. The etheric body of the woman dissolves easily after death and the male etheric body has the natural tendency to be conserved longer. The same applies also to Western and Eastern etheric bodies; globally speaking, the West is 'masculine' and the East 'feminine'. In this connection Rudolf Steiner adds that in America *only* female leaders can bring any good to social life, and that this can never happen in America through men.

Let us briefly review the timetable of our future evolution, in the light of what we said above. The mystery of the wound of sexuality and mortality, which leads either to ahrimanic or Michaelic immortality, will have to be resolved starting from the present age of Michael in the present fifth cultural epoch that will end in 3573, and in the coming sixth cultural epoch in 3573-5733. In the crucial time in the sixth and seventh millennia, a far-reaching spiritualization and healing of humanity and the earth must take place. At the same time, we will also be preparing the cataclysmic reunification of earth and the moon and the war of all against all that will end the fifth post-Atlantean age and change again the physical formation of the earth. Then the division of the sexes and the forces of sexuality as we know it, will also cease among those human beings who took into themselves the Christ impulse. In the sixth cultural epoch the first number six will have appeared on the clock of our evolution. After the war of all against all, in the sixth post-Atlantean age, the battle will have assumed astral-spiritual forms, because the division of humanity will be along purely moral lines and the evil race will have been incarnated in immoral physical bodies. When, in the sixth epoch of the sixth post-Atlantean age, the epoch of the opening of the seals, to speak in the language of Revelation, the sixth seal will be opened and resolved, the second and much more fatal number six will have appeared on the evolutionary clock. Before this time, most of the work of salvation must have achieved its goals. This must be prepared in the present age of Michael and the Second Coming and this is one of the main tasks of spiritual science in the twenty-first century.

The moment these apocalyptic events came to the light of clear supersensible perception and cognition at the transition between the end of last century and the beginning of the present century, was a significant victory of the Michaelic forces. It enabled Michael's forces, working in human hearts, to break through the deadlock of the entire twentieth century that had attained its culmination at the end of the century. This event opened an etheric path into his present impulse that flows from the second, middle century of his present age. Recall again how in the Mystery Dramas, Doctor Strader and Benedictus fight with Ahriman, and how, in the moment that Benedictus recognizes Ahriman, Ahriman says: 'Oh, I am seen and recognized for what I am! This spiritual gaze of recognition burns me like fire! I must escape this place!' And this signified an important victory of Benedictus over Ahriman, after many struggles, in which Strader's sacrifice played a significant role. As we showed above, this is connected to the remarkable destiny of Spicker-Strader and to the *genius loci* of this region. It was really a blessing of karma that allowed us to speak about these things here with the help of this *genius loci* in this place of healing. We will take with us the forces received here and carry them in our hearts as we travel to Inari in Lapland to commemorate the centenary of the burning of the first Goetheanum, which marked another gaping wound in the astral light of last century.

Then we will follow, during the centenary year of 1923, the spiritualization process of the flames that devoured the first Goetheanum, that led to the Christmas Foundation Conference in 1923-4, and then its further spiritualization through Rudolf Steiner's death in 1925 until 2025. We will not speak about 'centennial' and commemorate a quantity of dead historical time, while we only dance around the dead corpse left behind by the living spiritual event that took place 100 years ago. We will instead contemplate with our whole soul and heart what current spiritual scientific research reveals concerning its development in the etheric world from 1923-4-5 until 2023-4-5. If we don't merely repeat the same phrases and conventions, but rise up consciously—that is, spiritually—to grasp what took place in the etheric world between 1922 and 2022, 1923-4 and 2023-4, and between 1925 and 2025, the true meaning of the supersensible events of the three centennials of 1922-3-4-5 will light up in your consciousness. Then you will experience how it evolved and continues to evolve through the spiritual event of the twentieth century, as a living, growing and flowering spiritual event, ripening in the etheric world in the last 3x33 years, which must become part of the Michaelic stream on earth today and in the near future. Then we can begin to actualize its life-giving fruits on earth today and tomorrow.

It was the light radiating from the spiritual event of the twentieth century that has served us as a spiritual compass since the end of last century. You could say that when we were searching for the light of the new Christ impulse in the formidable darkness that enveloped and covered the earth in the 1980s and 90s, it appeared as a radiating North Star, the polar star, gleaming through this darkness, as a gentle glow of hope-giving light. This is the polar star of our evolution, the star of Christ, whose light was shining from the spiritual event of the twentieth century, often hardly seen from the earth, because of the dark cloud formations that thickened around it in the course of the twentieth century. Turning our gaze to this gleaming, flickering light, we oriented our work at the end of the century, searching for a pathway through the labyrinths of the apocalypse of the twentieth century. We wanted to find it again after we incarnated on earth; it illumined the narrow path with the spiritualized memory of the spiritual event of the twentieth century, to which the etheric Christ directed our spirit gaze.

Through the guiding light of this star, we could orient our work through the years to appraise how far we were from the goal of our work and how we could draw closer to its central axis, in our circling, spiralling path around and towards it. Let me draw this picture on the blackboard in this way. There, at the top is the spiritual polar star and the central axis around which the spiritual earth rotates. Before birth, we were united in this event, participating in the formation of the new Michaelic impulse as part of the formation of the embryo of the earthly-human Sun; as you search for this light on earth, you would remember it the more you spiritualize and resurrect old anthroposophy from the grave of civilization on the old, dying earth. In this light you can evaluate the work you have accomplished up to this day on earth, compare it with the spiritual event of the twentieth century, and you can realize how close or far you are from the central earth-sun-star axis.

Then toward the end of last century, you could experience that you were waking up and remembering this event, and how this spiritual memory became a present spiritual awareness and spiritual seeing, and you realized that the light of the radiating star above is actually the light of the new etheric Heaven, and you felt how under your feet, the new etheric Earth is rising up from below, answering the light of the new Heaven streaming from above; and you could experience the emergence of the earthly-human Sun-star, in which you live, move, and have your being. You can thus become realistic about the work on earth, because you could see: the goal that we are aiming at that shines, to begin with, as if from afar, as the polar star, is not at all far from you. It is not far above in the old heavens, nor in the depths of the old earth, but is so close to your heart, living and becoming here and now, embodied in your etheric head, heart and limbs. And what appeared to be, through the illusions of spatial perspective, far away, appears now to be the closest! What you are gazing at appears right here and now, and New Jerusalem lights up as the golden star of the heart of the new earthly-human Sun.

Therefore, when we soon gather physically under the North Pole, in Lapland, to celebrate the centennial of the burning of the first Goetheanum, we shall know: now we stand right here and now, under the North Star and Pole, and we feel the powerful spiritual streams of the vertical cosmic-earthly axis, passing right through us from above downward, through our bodies into the centre of the earth, and through the centre of the earth to the South Pole. You feel how it ascends upward from the South Pole through the centre of the earth and your body, to unite with the gleaming fiery light of the North Pole; and you feel how the two poles are connected by one vertical axial stream, and how our earthly humanity expands and embraces our planetary life through the wide circumference, and how it merges with our cosmic existence, in which the mysteries of the heights, the depths and the circumference unite and exchange their forces in the middle, where the heart of the earthly-human Sun and our etheric heart become one.

In this moment you are fully awake, spiritually, and you remember, you become aware, and you see the cosmic sunrise moment of the new Aurora, the fresh youthful dawn of the earthly-human Sun, shimmering and radiating with its magnificent auric colours, resounding with the most marvellous spiritual tones, in and through you, as it pierces through the crumbling ruins of the old earth below and lights up through the dark old heaven above; and you see how from above and below the New Heaven and Earth, the New Jerusalem, is taking shape in your earthly-human Sun hearts.

And then you know: now the spiritual event of the twentieth century is fully embodied on earth, now the rainbow bridge is completed, and the temple rises, because the time has come! 'Follow this good star,' said Rudolf Steiner at the end of the last lecture of the Christmas Foundation Conference, 'and if we prove to be worthy of this aim, we shall see that a good star will hold sway over what is willed from here. Follow this good star, my dear friends! We shall see whither the Gods will lead us by the light of this star:

> O Light Divine,
> O Sun of Christ!
> Warm Thou
> Our Hearts
> Enlighten Thou
> Our Heads.[43]

---

[43] Lecture of 1 January 1924 (GA 233).

Lecture 5

The Time Is At Hand!

Überlingen, 5 November 2022

As you would recall, Rudolf Steiner often said: Every time is a time of transition and change, the question is precisely what this particular transition means. Therefore, when we say that the present time is a time of great change, we must explain what *kind* of change is meant. In the same vein, I would like to say: the five years since 2017 have proved to be a very productive time of change, in which new and powerful impulses have been received from the spiritual world. I expressed this in the lecture cycle given in our school meeting in Sweden in 2019, published in the book, *The Twilight and Resurrection of Humanity*. And the aim of our lectures here is to continue to direct our gaze to this incoming Michaelic inspiration. We can introduce this subject if we turn our attention tonight to the following fact.

To characterize what is special about the present change, we can point out the fact that the three final 3x33 year-cycles of Rudolf Steiner's life and work are being completed. All the hundred-year cycles of Rudolf Steiner's earthly life and work are coming to closure, and also possible resurrection and rebirth. We have taken it as a special task, to concentrate on the three major events of his unfinished previous earthly life: the centenary of the burning of the first Goetheanum on New Year's Eve 1922, the Christmas Foundation Conference in 1923-4, and his premature death on 30 March, 1925. Naturally, we could have done the same with each year of his life and theosophical-anthroposophical work. Since 2002 each year was a centenary of his work in the previous century. And now, in 2022, 2023-4, and 2025, we can experience the

The Time Is At Hand! 103

meaning of the completion of the ultimate 3x33 year-cycle of his spiritual work as a whole. And this means something, not only for us but also for his connection with the current work on earth and if he will be able to return to earth in this century.

I can tell you from my experience how productive the inner co-creating of these cycles is. In the 1980s, I started to follow and activate in my soul, whatever I could from what Rudolf Steiner wrote and did a century ago. I found it very fruitful for my spiritual work. Each year I studied what he wrote in his autobiography about his life and work a hundred years ago during the 1880s and 90s. I made it into a kind of personal reversed cultus, in which I would consummate each particular study in a meditative praxis and offer the results to the higher worlds. I did it also at the end of each year, looking back at the year as a whole, as far as this was possible in the documentation of Rudolf Steiner's life in the 1880s and 90s, in Vienna and Weimar, and in the first years in Berlin before and after the turn of the century. And I did the same when he started the theosophical-anthroposophical work in 1901-2, and in 2001-2, I could also study the lectures he gave on the same day a century ago. As a matter of fact, the practice of this 3x33 year rhythm on a daily and annual basis brought many good results. I started it before Lindenberg wrote his more external chronicle, and also before I could read Wachsmuth's and Bock's books. I mention this to emphasize the meaning of what is *coming to completion, transformation, and rebirth,* in the next three years, 2022-2025, through 3x33 year-cycle of birth, death and resurrection.

When you understand the significance of this cycle, you would recall the words with which Rudolf Steiner ended the year 1917, the most decisive historical year of the last century. He explicated the meaning of the 33 and 3x33 years rhythm, based on the esoteric meaning behind the Catholic credo, *Et incarnatus est de spiritu sancto ex Maria virgine,* namely, *He was incarnated through the Holy Ghost out of the Virgin Mary and was made man*. This signifies the sacred rhythm of birth, death and resurrection imprinted by the life of Jesus Christ in the historical stream of time, active in human evolution ever since the Mystery of Golgotha.[44]

In *The Twilight and Resurrection of Humanity* you can study more closely the meaning of this rhythm for our work. In just a few words we can say that 33 years is the earthly signature of the time of the life of Jesus Christ, which begins with Jesus's birth and culminates with Jesus Christ's death and resurrection. Any seed or child of a new deed, thought, and will impulse, to the extent that it is born from the Holy Spirit, namely, as a free impulse from the depth of the human soul and the spiritual world, will grow and develop in the world for the next 33 years, in which its forces of freedom and love will be permeated and transformed by the life stream flowing from Golgotha. And after 33 years, what remained perishable, all too human in it, will die out and its spiritual essence will be resurrected to new life. For 33 years this deed developed in Christ's living time stream, active in the etheric aura of the earth, and if we perceive this etheric aura, we can also perceive this rhythm. It is there, and what we did 33 years ago and developed in a living way since then, will be resurrected today, and what we think, feel and do today will find its fulfilment after the next 33 years, and its truth will be reborn, rejuvenated, and spiritualized further. And Rudolf Steiner indicates that after 3 x 33 years have passed, this cycle will have attained an even greater degree of spiritualization. This is the essence of the spiralling, self-enhancing, growing and metamorphosing evolutionary stream of any true spiritual impulse.

In essence, this process of spiritualization spread out during 33 years and 3x33 years, is what we accomplish, in a nutshell, in each true meditation, and if we practise our

---

[44] Lectures of 23 & 26 December 1917 (GA 180).

meditations in this way, we will experience that they immerse us in the etheric aura of the earth, and we will experience how the fruits of each meditation are fertilized and spiritualized, from day to day, year and decade, by the life-time of the etheric Christ. He will be there, by our side, actively demonstrating, in His appearance, words and deeds, this mystery. He will take up our loving offer, and will give it back to us, purified from our egotism and spiritualized further. This practice will also open the spiritual eyes of our etheric heart to perceive the historical development of His 33-year life cycles.

Rudolf Steiner said: 'For all things in historical evolution rise from the grave in a changed form after 33 years by the power that is connected to the most sacred redemptive gift, which humanity received through the Mystery of Golgotha.' And this means for every human thought and deed that is done, even the humblest, if this deed or thought contains even a tiny element of the Holy Spirit within it—the spirit of freedom and truthful love—it will be resurrected from the grave of historical time, the grave of modern civilization, in a new form after the 33 years and will continue to evolve in the next 33 year cycles. As you plant a seed in the earth, the seed may naturally contain many different forces; some will rot and die, but others will bring forth the whole plant. What is pure and virgin, that is, truthful, is the Christ essence of this deed. Each thought that we bring forth, each deed that we do through the spirit of true freedom and love, contains concentrated Christ essence in it, to the extent that it comes from this pure source of our heart and mind, and it will grow and develop, and after 3x33 years it will attain a certain fruition, a certain flowering and harvest of its highest potential and quality, and the production of many new and highly fertile spirit seeds.

Rudolf Steiner means, therefore, that a truthful seed of thought or a deed takes a whole human generation of 33 years to ripen. When it has ripened it goes on working in historic evolution for the next 33 years, and then for 33 years more. After 3x33 years, he says, the intensity of an impulse planted in the stream of living historical time, can be fully permeated and transformed by the life forces of the etheric Christ, working in the etheric aura of the earth. And if it increases its resurrection forces through three generations, through a whole century, its essence will be resurrected and spiritualized to the highest degree, provided—this is naturally the narrow eye of this time needle—that it will find the suitably fertile soil in richly prepared human hearts, in which it can be resurrected and reborn.

Now, this is precisely what is so significant about the present years, because if we are attentive to the etheric Christ impulse working through our etheric hearts, if we are constantly resurrecting with its forces what Rudolf Steiner accomplished 3x33 years ago, we may participate in this great event of 'die and become', of resurrection from the grave of history. In this way we resurrect to new life, in our purest thoughts and deeds and feelings, what Rudolf Steiner thought and did 3x33 years ago, which was born of the Holy Spirit of freedom and love, the spirit of Michael and Christ. If we have connected our best Christ-permeated forces with this stream through the years, we would experience its culmination and transformation after 3x33 years. At this time, it becomes especially powerful and fruitful, at the culmination of the whole cycle of a century. And when a group of people gather together, as we try to do, and learn this science, art and cultus of historical resurrection, it can resurrect the living seed that Rudolf Steiner created and planted in the grave of historical time 3x33 years ago in our free etheric hearts from its present grave. Then it will rise up through our communal thinking, feeling and will, our love, devotion, and empowerment of each other, and we will be able to consciously grasp its present historical rebirth, metamorphosis, and transformation, *and what it is striving to accomplish as its next stage of development on earth.* But we must resurrect and recreate it in ourselves. If we do so, actively and creatively with devotion and gratitude, we will experience the living culmination of this sacred Christ rhythm in 2022, 2023-4 and 2025.

This is the reason we should become profoundly enthusiastic about this development in recent years. I believe that those of you who were attentive to the development of our work even only since 2017, could have felt this 3x33 resurrection impulse very clearly. Not because this is a date on the calendar that one feels obliged to commemorate in an external way as people do in our time. We are inspired because we experience its living pulse, breathing and flowing with the etheric current of Christ's and Michael's threefold heartbeat, described in *The Twilight and Resurrection of Humanity*. It is a real experience for us, and is an organic, spiritual continuation and enhancement of the work we have been doing in recent years. And maybe for the first time a feeling may arise in our hearts, telling us: Oh, we did many things in the last ten years and now we may feel that some of them were in line with this resurrection impulse, others perhaps not so much. But over time our efforts were more refined and in tune with the new impulses of Christ and Michael, and our etheric hearts began to think, perceive, feel and will, what is streaming so abundantly in recent years from the spiritual world.

Let me illustrate this by drawing on the blackboard. The spiritual impulse that connects the spiritual and physical worlds is indicated in this vertical line, around which we were gathered, working with it in the circumference, circling and spiralling along its vertical thrust; and with each year we laboured in tracing the spiralling curve, we drew closer to the central axis, rising higher to its flower and deepening our roots in its foundations. And the peripheral work drew closer and closer to the central stream, until the moment could come in which our work and the spiritual stream could get closer and closer, flow through each other, and finally unite into one, striving to bring about the flowering together of the three centenary events. And this etheric rhythmic breathing between the vertical central stream and the spiralling periphery, is the real esoteric dynamic that brings to consciousness the meaning of the three centenary events of 2022, 2023-4 and 2025, and opens the portal of the coming years and decades, through which the new, future inspiration of Michael is flowing.

You could say that this is a lofty goal, to strive to experience how our humble work and the new revelation of the etheric Christ and the new impulse of Michael are coming together. But this must be perceived. It must be experienced, not auto-suggested, until one would be able to say: Now these are no longer two separate streams. They were two neighbouring, perhaps closely related streams, but still *different* streams, but now they are one.[45] The moment has come for the mutual essence exchange and merging of both, and this means something not only for us. It has an objective significance for the development of the stream of Michael in the second century of his present age.

When you experience this, you may say to yourself: It seems that it was worthwhile to work hard to achieve this goal in recent decades. You come to the point in which you feel: I am getting closer to the main thrust of the real spiritual impulse of the present age. Until this moment—with all due respect, dear friends, to all our dear members attending our meeting and watching us in Zoom around the world—we should have felt: Indeed, we were getting closer, but it was not yet the real thing. Such essence exchange of centre and periphery was not yet experienced; the clear distance between idea and ideal, between ideal and deed, could still be perceived; it was not really coming to full merging. We were still a little bit too early or too late, too much to the left

---

[45] In the third chapter of *The Three Meetings*, I described another aspect of this merging as 'the Platonic-Aristotelian essence exchange at the end of the twentieth century'.

or to the right, too high or too low. And though our compass never veered off the path traced by our guiding star, and we could consistently reorient ourselves back towards the centre, it was still this coming and going, drawing closer and getting again further away. It was never really getting so close to the goal that you could actually feel how this merging might take place.

Naturally, for a community to grow up like this, some time is required, because to unite a whole community with this highest spiritual stream, is very different than doing it by yourself; you must take each member into account, and have to go through certain developments, attain certain purifications, await some challenging self-overcomings. It takes years until slowly, by degrees, the communal work becomes a robust and transparent chalice for the real spirit. And it was the loyalty to the ever living, ever recurring, meeting with the etheric Christ, on the one hand, and the loyalty to His ever living and recurring current planetary-cosmic revelation, on the other hand, that has served us since the end of last century as our trustworthy guide on the path, directed and mentored by Michael.

This is the moment in which we feel that the construction of the etheric bridge of continuity of consciousness has become firm and stable enough, and it allows us to perceive the convergence of our peripheral work and the spiralling central impulse, that bridges and unites the new Heaven and Earth, revealing the rising temple of the earthly-human Sun. This moment is really the resurrection and rebirth of the human-cosmic seed that Rudolf Steiner planted 3x33 years ago, the new-born seed of the future stream of Michael, forming in our midst. The most potent and fruitful spiritual seeds that Rudolf Steiner planted on the earth in 1922, 1923, 1924, 1925, that could not develop on earth, that bore the strongest forces of sacrifice and redemption in the etheric world during the spiritual events of last century, are awakened, activated, and are beginning to grow *on earth* after 3x33 years.

In this context, it is important to recall the promise that Rudolf Steiner made to the spiritual world, which means, concretely speaking, to his mentor Michael, when he decided to reverse the ancient esoteric law of leadership, that decreed that the initiate should not be involved in the physical, human and social realization of this teaching. Out of his free moral intuition, his human freedom and love, he decided to initiate and lead a social organization on earth, the new Anthroposophical Society. The essence of this promise was embodied in the formation and laying of the Foundation Stone of Love in the Christmas Foundation Conference in 1923-4. What exactly was the nature of this promise and what does it mean today, after 3x33 years?

The promise was that, as he assumes before the spiritual world his role as the teacher of free humanity, in the age of the consciousness soul, he takes full responsibility for the consequences of what ordinary, uninitiated humans will do with this free decision. The results of their acceptance or rejection of this impulse will fall on him. As we saw above, the fact that this new impulse was not accepted was already perceived in real time in the spiritual world by the soul of Moltke, and naturally also by Rudolf Steiner, already in January 1924. Marie Steiner could testify to this 20 years later in 1944. She writes that the Christmas Foundation Conference 'represents the mightiest endeavour of a teacher of mankind to lift his contemporaries out of their own small selves and awaken in them a conscious will to be allowed to become tools serving the wise guides of the universe. Yet at the same time this Christmas Foundation Conference is also bound up with something infinitely tragic. For we cannot but admit: we were called, but we were not chosen. We were incapable of responding to the call, as further developments

The Time Is At Hand! 111

showed...the outcome revealed what it meant for Dr Steiner to take our karma upon himself.'[46]

In other words, Rudolf Steiner had to shoulder the karmic consequences that resulted from the rejection of his free moral deed, and this meant that he could not complete his mission and had to leave the earth on 30 March, 1925. His call, which was Michael's cosmic-earthly call, *Menschen mögen es hören,* was not heard, nor taken into the hearts and realized among his pupils. What he gave, and what Michael offered humanity so abundantly through him as a positive response to his decision, returned to its spiritual source, and continued its development in the etheric world through the spiritual event of the twentieth century, while humanity and the earth fell ever deeper into the abyss of the grave of civilization.

This means, dear friends, that our task in the three centenary events is to demonstrate that after the resurrection cycle of 3x33 years has been completed, we hear the *present* cosmic-earthly call of Michael, take it actively into our free and loving etheric hearts, and act upon it creatively. This must be the human answer, if we experience in the present the active fulfilment of Christ's cycle of time of 3x33 years. If also after a century, the active human answer will not be heard in the spiritual world, and the lagging of humanity behind the schedule of the age of Michael will continue to increase, destructive consequences will grow. If the creative answer to Michael's present call is not realized by the middle of the century, as Rudolf Steiner warned already in 1922, 'The Michael Age would go by. Michael would retire from his rulership and would bring this message to the Gods: Humanity desires to separate itself from the Gods.'[47] We are very close to this dangerously critical moment, dear friends! It is there-

---

[46] Foreword to the first German Edition of the Christmas Foundation Conference, 1944 (GA 260).
[47] Lecture of 17 December 1922 (GA 219).

fore up to us, to wake ourselves up, make today our own free resolve, and answer this cosmic-earthly call, here and now; this cannot be achieved, naturally, with mere thoughts and feelings, even if we believe, subjectively, that we are truly devoted and loyal, but only through creative spiritual and communal *deeds*. We can only answer Michael's *Wort* (word) with our honest human *Ant-wort* (answer), and respond enthusiastically to his call. But this means in real life praxis, to lift up, joyfully, the sacrifice of our little egos, give up our vanities and ambitions, jealousies and fears, that have caused in the last century endless conflicts with each other, and fill our free etheric heart with the strongest love to ourselves and our companions. Only in this manner can humans *demonstrate* the real praxis of spiritual remembrance, mindfulness, and seeing, and give honest expression to their creative, serious, festive response-ability. As you know, even today, as we speak at the end of 2022, humans still do not want to hear it, to take it into their etheric hearts, transform their egotism, unite in true love with their companions, and build the long-awaited future community of true spiritual brotherhood.

This can only be done if the significance of the *supersensible* events of the twentieth and twenty-first centuries is grasped and cultivated now on the earth, in fully awakened human consciousness, and implemented in the formation of the new community, school and movement of Michael. If we do so, our present answer would resound clearly and creatively: *The time is at hand!*

This has been our main task since Easter 1975. When we celebrate in 2025 the centenary of the death of Rudolf Steiner, 7x7 Jubilee years and the fiftieth anniversary of this impulse would have been fulfilled. And this can be increasingly experienced in our recent work. Not only in the deepening of the spiritual contents of the work, though indeed the revelations from the spiritual world have greatly increased in recent years; but even more you could experience it in the changing and deepening intimate community mood and *Stimmung*, the struggle to articulate the new spiritual language to express the fact that the new impulses are flowing through the etheric heart. You could have felt, I believe, that Goethe's life maxim—'The "what" is important, but more important is the "how"'—has become increasingly true among us. This new language of the heart confirms the signs of the time that appear in the heavens of the earthly-human Sun, signalling that we are on the right path. This expresses the human aspect, the new soul and communal life, through the new heart forces of love and devotion, gratitude and reverence, and we would feel how blessed we are with grace that we could find this path at all, that we know about it, and can humbly practise it. Thus, the soul aspect resonates with the mighty cosmic impulses, while we gather together to form the nucleus of the new Michaelic community on earth.

This open and active, enthusiastic, and creative soil of the heart and all the forces of the soul, is what Michael and his hosts are searching for. This is what this impulse was preparing in the etheric world since 1925: to return to the earth and reincarnate again in the twenty-first century. Because it can only return if this heart-shaped and heart-filled community is ready to receive it.

We can picture it like this, by drawing on the blackboard a star above the middle point of last century, shining in the etheric world above the black clouds that engulfed the earth. Its light signifies the spiritual event of the twentieth century and the supersensible Michaelic conference in the late 40s and beginning of the 1950s, described in *The Twilight and Resurrection of Humanity*. It radiates in the etheric world in the middle between the hopeful beginning and abysmal end of last century. To the left, on earth below in 1923-4, the Christmas Foundation Conference is taking place, and a year and a half later Rudolf Steiner and anthroposophy leave the earth and continue to evolve in the etheric world. When Rudolf Steiner dies, the new Christmas Conference impulse and the school of Michael goes with him to the etheric world. In the etheric world during the darkest time between 1930 and 1950, the mighty spiritual event takes place as a deed of redemption, as sacrificial operation to save the possibility of future human evolution. And now picture on the right side, towards the end of the century, how the dramatic question which loomed so large in the etheric world, is heard on earth: Will this impulse be able to come down to earth again? Will it be able to find at least a few souls who would awaken spiritually on earth, to grasp it and resurrect old anthroposophy from its grave and receive the new Michaelic impulse on earth?

At the middle of the century, the two streams were farthest from each other. And you feel this impulse burning in your etheric hearts, because you know: they *must* get closer to each other and merge at the end of the century. For this end, the new plan of Michael was drafted in the 1950s, described in *The Twilight and Resurrection of Humanity*. But on earth you must find your way to this new supersensible plan. It lights up for the first time in Easter 1975. For the first time the two streams, the earthly and supersensible streams of Michael, begin to touch each other, and begin their path of getting closer to one another. From that moment on, the struggle on earth was to spiritualize old anthroposophy on earth with the forces of the new Christ impulse; to fertilize it with the new forces of Michael and resurrect it from the grave of civilization. And in the 1980s and 90s the two streams were increasingly united to create the third stream; their offspring, born of their union and the resurrection stream could begin to develop.

If you look back to this point of time in Easter 1975, almost 50 years ago, you could see how the first spark of the new Christ impulse from the etheric world was kindled on the earth. You could see—and this is significant for us—how in Easter 1975 the golden star of Golgotha comes to life in the purple-bluish aura of Jerusalem, how it is awakened, how it lights up! This was the year when the first incarnation of the new Christ-Michael impulse, prepared in the etheric world from 1925 until 1955, was perceived, which was descending in 1955-1975 from the life before birth, from the spiritual event of the twentieth century. And since then, gradually, this impulse developed, struggling naturally through many obstacles placed on its path by the ahrimanic zeitgeist and the approaching unification of the forces of the two apocalyptic Beasts in 1998. But if you look back carefully with an Imaginative gaze, you will see how at that moment the supersensible Michaelic stream began to assimilate, spiritualize and awaken to new life the dead bones of old anthroposophy, which Rudolf Steiner embodied on earth until 1925. The new and old streams grew gradually closer to one another and fertilized each other in the 70s, 80s and 90s, until they could merge and give birth to the third stream. And when my first books were published, *The Spiritual Event of the Twentieth Century* in 1993, and *The New Experience of the Supersensible* in 1995, the first fruit of their union, the third stream, could come to light. With this resurrection stream, in which the merged force of the new and old anthroposophy was developing, one could create the stable etheric bridge of spiritual memory and continuity of consciousness, cross the turbulent abyss of the threshold of the twentieth and twenty-first centuries, and enter with it into the third millennium. One could begin in the first decade of the twenty-first century to build a new Michaelic community, base it on the resurrection and spiritualization of the most elementary foundations of spiritual science, and search for souls who would open their hearts to receive the new Christ impulse and grasp the new forces of Michael with active and creative fiery enthusiasm.

If we accomplish this, we would be able to say that this really new Michaelic impulse, the seed of which was laid in 1923-4, but couldn't germinate and grow on earth then, after it went through 3 times 33 years of metamorphosis in the etheric world, can now be truly grasped by human hearts on earth, who are energetically and creatively answering its call. If these souls are found, and the new community of united etheric hearts can be formed, the new seed of the coming Michaelic impulse of the twenty-first century would be planted and cultivated in a healthy way.

Speaking in the language of Chapter 12 of Revelation, this would mean that the old mother Anthroposophia, who fled to the desert in 1925, persecuted by the ahrimanic dragon, will be fertilized by the young, supersensible Anthroposophia, and be resurrected to new life; it would regain its eternal virginity, grow young again and the two mothers: the old, earth-bound Anthroposophia and the young spiritual being of Anthroposophia, would unite again, hopefully to remain united for a longer time on earth than was possible in their short union in 1924. So, the two anthroposophical mothers, separated in Michaelmas 1924 when Rudolf Steiner gave his last address, would unite again for the first time on earth, through the new Christ revelation and the new Michaelic impulse; and what was created in the Spiritual Event of the twentieth century would find its true embodiment on earth. And the new-born Christ child, the true human 'I' who was born in the Christmas Foundation Conference but who had to be hastily taken up to the spiritual world to rescue it from Ahriman and the apocalyptic Beasts in the twentieth century, will be able to incarnate and be born for the first time in free human hearts, to grow and develop into earthly maturity, as the basis of the new community and the etheric bridge that must be built by the middle of the century.

The Christ child, the true son of Anthroposophia and Michael, was born on earth in 1923-4, as you can see in the image on the blackboard. He is the true 'I', the spiritual human Ego of 'the human being Anthroposophia', born after 21 years of anthroposophical development in 1902-1923. This 'I' who came down, incorporated in the spiritualized forces of the burned down Goetheanum, was born in the Christmas Foundation Conference, but could find on earth only closed hearts and no earthly home, precisely like his higher archetype 2000 years ago, in Bethlehem. It could stay on the earth from Christmas 1923 until Michaelmas 1924, through the being of Rudolf Steiner, and was rescued with his spiritual mother and carried into the spiritual world. This divine-human child, our true human-cosmic self, conceived by mother Anthroposophia and Michael, *must* be able to return to the earth after the full Christed time cycle of 3x33 years has been fulfilled, if humanity and the earth are to survive in the present age of Michael. This can only happen, however, if after 3x33 years some human souls would have heard the call, resounding from 1923-4 through the Spiritual Event of the twentieth century, from 1975 until 2025, and would have answered, with all the forces of their etheric hearts: Yes, *Menschen haben es gehört!* in 2022, 2023-4, and 2025. This answer must resound powerfully, creatively: Yes, in fact some souls are now answering it! Humans have actualized it in their etheric hearts, humans are actualizing it in their loving deeds in the formation of the etheric bridge and the temple of the earthly-human Sun! And because we are actually practising it, we would also be able to exclaim, with some justification: *Es ist wirklich an der Zeit,* the time is indeed at hand!

Dear friends, this is what I wanted to say in our last lecture, to prepare our hearts to actualize in the right mood the coming three centenaries. I also wanted to express my conviction that we can be very enthusiastic, serious and joyful about the time in which we live today on earth. And we can continue our preparations and our work in the coming three years, with holy Michaelic enthusiasm and energy, perseverance, and festivity, to intensify our growth and become productive inwardly and outwardly. And we may feel that as the work becomes livelier, we become younger and more creative. The sign of this growing younger will be that we become more hopeful, trusting, brotherly and sisterly, and more joyful in our community-building work. That is how we prepare the sacred marriage of the new Heaven and Earth, with feelings of gratitude and reverence, feeling this absolutely unique *Stimmung* of devotion to the significant historical time in which we live. And when we truly feel it, we would say: OK, because this festive mood is well prepared, I am allowed to be happy! Michaelic happiness is justified, is allowed, if one has worked to attain it for many years and decades, actualizing in this creation all the forces of one's heart and soul in daily life.

It is earnest, sacred work and it must culminate in a festive mood of celebration, the beginning of the cosmic cultus and spiritual communion of humanity, about which Rudolf Steiner spoke in the almost completed first Goetheanum on New Year's Eve 1922, while the flames of fire were already burning between its mighty wooden walls. This cosmic cultus and spiritual communion of humanity, spiritualized in the flames and rising as a sacred sacrifice to the cosmos, returned as a mighty new Michaelic inspiration, which Rudolf Steiner transformed at the end of 1923 into the Foundation Stone of Love in the Christmas Foundation Conference.

Let us be worthy of this immense sacrifice offered to humanity, the earth, and the spiritual worlds 3x33 years ago, and let it be joyfully resurrected in our etheric hearts as the fiery flames of the new cosmic cultus and spiritual communion of humanity—the future festival in which the guiding Michaelic spiritual beings will actually work together with fully conscious humans on the earth, to complete the bridge of spiritual memory and continuity of consciousness and the brotherhood and sisterhood of the present age of Michael. Then, indeed, we may say a third time: *The time is at hand!* But what exactly is this time, that is now at hand?

> As soon as the words [of the Green Snake] resound in the temple: I want to sacrifice myself! The old man shouts: The time has come!

The words of the old man, the time has come, point to the distant future when the whole of humanity has attained their maturity. Then the time has come when the temple rises up above the river, when all of humanity takes part in wisdom, in the initiation which was otherwise given to a few people only in the temples, in the abysses.[48]

Our time, 3x33 years after the Christmas Foundation Conference, is the beginning of this future time, in which the first *mortals* answer the call of the gods, *uninitiated* humans construct the bridge of the continuity of consciousness, and lay the foundation stone of the earthly-human Sun temple.

And this is the deeper meaning of our work in the coming 2020s and 30s, dear friends: to be 'the preparers of the preparers', as Rudolf Steiner said in the lectures about the apocalypse in Nuremberg in 1908. We must become the first mortals to construct the bridge and let the open temple of humanity, the new mysteries, burned in 1922-3-4, rise again in our hearts, graced by the new revelation of the etheric Christ and the new impulse of Michael. And if our response-ability is honest and creative, it will be taken up by Rudolf Steiner and presented to Michael, as the firstborn fruit of what humans can accomplish with their forces in his present age, and Michael will be able to represent humanity in the council of the gods, telling them that 'During my Age, people have raised their [spiritualized thinking] to the supersensible...and we can therefore accept people again, for they have united their thought with ours.'[49]

---

[48] Lecture of 16 February 1905 (GA 53).
[49] Lecture of 17 December 1922 (GA 219).

Quoted Volumes from Rudolf Steiner's Collected Works

English titles are given where published translations are available.

CW 53	*Ursprung und Ziel des Menschen*
CW 104	*The Apolcalypse of St John*
CW 112	*The Gospel of St John and Its Relation to the Other Gospels*
CW 118	*The Second Coming of Christ*
CW 175	*Building Stones for an Understanding of the Mystery of Golgotha*
CW 178	*Secret Brotherhoods*
CW 180	*Ancient Myths and the New Isis Mystery*
CW 181	*Dying Earth and Living Cosmos*
CW 190	*Past and Future Impulses in Societal Events*
CW 209	*Der Mensch in Zusammenhang mit dem Kosmos 9: Nordische und mitteleuropäische Geistimpulse. Das Fest der Erscheinung Christi*
CW 217a	*Youth and the Etheric Heart*
CW 219	*Man and the World of Stars*
CW 233	*World History in the Light of Anthroposophy*
CW 237	*Karmic Relationships*, Vol. 3
CW 239	*Karmic Relationships*, Vol. 5 (see also Vol. 7)
CW 240	*Karmic Relationships*, Vol. 6
CW 260	*The Christmas Conference for the Founding of the General Anthroposophical Society 1923/1924*

CW 266/1   *Esoteric Lessons 1904-1909*

CW 266/2   *Esoteric Lessons 1910-1912*

CW 266/3   *Esoteric Lessons 1913 -1923*

CW 346   *The Book of Revelation and the Work of the Priest*

For English-language titles contact Rudolf Steiner Press, UK (www.rudolfsteinerpress.com) or SteinerBooks, USA (www.steinerbooks.org)

A note from the publisher

For more than a quarter of a century, **Temple Lodge Publishing** has made available new thought, ideas and research in the field of spiritual science.

Anthroposophy, as founded by Rudolf Steiner (1861-1925), is commonly known today through its practical applications, principally in education (Steiner-Waldorf schools) and agriculture (biodynamic food and wine). But behind this outer activity stands the core discipline of spiritual science, which continues to be developed and updated. True science can never be static and anthroposophy is living knowledge.

Our list features some of the best contemporary spiritual-scientific work available today, as well as introductory titles. So, visit us online at **www.templelodge.com** and join our emailing list for news on new titles.

If you feel like supporting our work, you can do so by buying our books or making a direct donation (we are a non-profit/ charitable organisation).

office@templelodge.com